Internet Resources
for
Economic Educators

Internet Resources for Economic Educators

by

Richard Upjohn and Holt Ruffin

National Council on Economic Education

Center for Civil Society International

Printed in the United States of America

Library of Congress Cataloging-in-Publication Data
Upjohn, Richard
Internet Resources for Economic Educators / by Richard Upjohn and M. Holt Ruffin

p. cm.
ISBN 1-891565-00-1

1. Web sites for economic educators. 2. Electronic mailing lists for economic educators. 3. Web sites for economic educators in Russian, Ukrainian and other languages.

Preface

If the idea of civil society implies a high level of public-spirited activity by individuals willing to give freely of their time and creative talents, this book stands as a symbol of the vitality of civil society on the Internet. For the reader will find inside these pages many examples of well-crafted, useful (and occasionally even humorous!) Web sites and electronic mailing lists which were created and are maintained by such public-spirited individuals. These essentially represent large donations of "human capital" for the common good.

Internet Resources for Economic Educators is an effort to share this wealth. It is one result of a long-term project of the National Council on Economic Education, funded by the Office of Educational Research and Improvement, U.S. Department of Education, designed to train economic educators living in the transition economies of the countries of the former Soviet Union, Baltic States and Central Europe. The book is initially being translated into Russian for use by these educators, and parts of the publication were specifically written with them in mind.

However, as a quick glance at the material contained in *Internet Resources for Economic Educators* will reveal, the great majority of it will be of use to economic educators throughout the U.S. and, indeed, throughout the world. Undoubtedly, those who do use the book will find some areas for improvement or will have specific additions to suggest for possible next editions. The authors encourage these users to forward any such suggestions to them at the Center for Civil Society International.

—*Richard Upjohn and Holt Ruffin*
Center for Civil Society International
2929 NE Blakeley Street
Seattle, WA 98105 USA
ccsi@u.washington.edu

Acknowledgments

Earlier drafts of this publication were shown to a number of economic educators. The authors wish to thank especially Professors Joyce Gleason, Kim Sosin, and Michelle Mason Winston, all of the University of Nebraska, and Ed Dolan, director of the American Institute for Business and Economics in Moscow, for their helpful comments and suggestions. We are also grateful to research assistants Alyssa Deutschler and Michelle Fuqua for their contributions to various sections of *Internet Resources for Economic Educators*.

Funding for this publication was provided by the National Council on Economic Education, under a grant from the U.S. Department of Education, Office of Educational Research and Improvement.

Table of Contents

Introduction

We are in the midst of an information revolution which can be compared with the development of moveable metal type in the 15th century. The first revolution led to mass publishing and universal literacy in many countries of the world, with enormous consequences for society. The current revolution is making vast information resources universally accessible to anybody with a relatively inexpensive computer and telephone line—with equally vast consequences for nations and societies around the world. The name of this revolution is the Internet.

The Internet is a network of networks. If two people use two computers which are linked by a cable and able to share files and information back and forth, they have created the most simple kind of network. Computer networks can consist of a few personal computers linked together this way in one or two rooms...or thousands of computers in different cities linked together through super-powerful "server" computers, which act as centralized data and computation centers. Government agencies, large corporations, airline reservation systems, and scientific organizations are examples of some of the institutions today which make use of large networks of computers linking millions of people across many cities, and even many nations.

The National Council on Economic Education and Center for Civil Society International, co-publishers of this resource, are both committed to the growth of economic literacy worldwide and to using the new communications technologies to this end. NCEE was founded in 1949 to advance the knowledge and understanding of economic principles among young people from kindergarten through senior high school. Its programs annually help more than 120,000 teachers in the U. S. to teach economic concepts to over 7 million students.

With significant assistance from the U. S. Department of Education, Office of Educational Research and Improvement, as well as from a number of Soros Foundations and the Amoco Foundation, NCEE in recent years launched an "**Economics**International" initiative. This program has helped partners in the emerging "market democracies" of the former Soviet Union and central and eastern Europe to reform their educational systems and programs for the difficult transition away from command economies. **Economics**International has accomplished this through a variety of activities including training programs, materials development and translation, and study tours. This publication is one example of the materials we have been able to produce with the support of a generous grant from the Department of Education.

Center for Civil Society International, established in 1992, publishes books, maintains an active World Wide Web site, and produces other resources devoted to providing information to the general public about a wide variety of projects such as NCEE's. In 1996, together with the University of Washington Press, CCSI published *The Post-Soviet Handbook: A Guide to Grassroots Organizations and Internet Resources in the New Independent States*. In this project, CCSI has been pleased to collaborate with NCEE in the development of this important new resource, *The Internet for Economic Educators*. We hope that individuals and institutions involved in economic education throughout the former Soviet bloc will find material in these pages that will help them in their tasks.

It scarcely needs to be pointed out that nations with high levels of unemployment and low levels of productivity are unlikely to develop into stable and democratic societies. Further, in this age of global trade and development, it is difficult for nations to join international economic institutions without demonstrated adherence to certain basic market-oriented economic institutions and practices. For this, nations emerging from former command economic systems, often need not only a deep change in national policies, but also a broad campaign of public education. The latter requires everything from the development of new curricula in schools and universities to the training, and re-training, of talented and dedicated professionals in the existing pools of teachers. *The Internet for Economic Educators* was developed to assist in this vitally important educational restructuring process in the nations of central and eastern Europe and the former Soviet Union.

How to Use This Guide

With this guide we have sought to identify a number of resources available through the Internet likely to be of interest to economic educators in the former Soviet bloc. Users should think of the resources identified in the pages that follow as excellent starting points from which they can begin their own search for those resources or applications which will best fit their needs or opportunities. The Internet is too vast for even a book focused on the resources it affords economic educators to claim to be comprehensive. But precisely because these resources are so extensive, just to begin looking can be a daunting task for those not very accustomed to "cyberspace. " Our hope is that a guide such as this will be of special value to novice or moderately-experienced Internet users, helping them to go online and discover the great materials that are accessible at the click of a finger. (Oh, well, a few clicks of a finger!)

The Internet is an inexpensive, powerful tool that can significantly assist the development of economic education worldwide. It strengthens communications and coordination between economic educators in countries where postal services are too slow or unreliable. Millions of people today use the Internet for e-mail, which is still by far its most popular application. E-mail connections—as opposed to full Internet access (meaning the World Wide Web)—are normally very inexpensive. In principle, with just simple e-mail access, educators as far apart as California and Ukraine can exchange experiences, curricular ideas, practical advice, and so on...all at little cost and without delays.

As more and more people gain access to the Internet, it also offers an increasingly appealing alternative to traditional print publishing. It takes relatively little additional work or money to turn a piece of text into a "page" on the World Wide Web, accessible by a readership that potentially numbers in the millions. It is turning into something of an art to design one's new "Web site" in such a way that it is found by Internet "surfers" who did not previously know about it, but in principle any individual can reach millions of people today through an Internet Web site.

The very best way for economic educators to appreciate the potential of the Internet is to get connected, go online, follow your curiosity, and explore. The 'net is best appreciated through such a process of exploration. The online world is full of information and resources that will reward the curious and strengthen the enterprising. For those of you who are already online, we hope this guide will nevertheless contain much that is new to you. If you are not online already, we hope the guide will stimulate your curiosity and encourage you to get connected. The staffs of our respective organizations stand ready to assist you in accessing the world-wide resources for professionals in the field of economic education!

Patricia Elder
National Council on Economic Education
New York, NY

Holt Ruffin
Center for Civil Society International
Seattle, WA

Internet Sites

This section describes a variety of sites on the World Wide Web with files or documents of interest to economic educators. It begins with clearinghouses—that is, sites which have a great variety of resources in many areas, making them excellent starting points for economic educators beginning to explore what the Internet has to offer. In selecting each particular site, we have been guided by the quality of materials to be found there, the clarity of its organization, and by evidence that the site is updated regularly and otherwise well maintained.

The technical name for an Internet address is Uniform Resource Locator or URL. (It is the series of characters beginning with "http://...") Internet addresses change from time to time, but if they do, Web site managers usually make sure—at least for a few months—that Internet browsers who use the old URL will get a page indicating the change of address and giving the new URL.

Clearinghouses

National Council on Economic Education

http://www.nationalcouncil.org/

The sponsor of this publication, the National Council on Economic Education, is the leading source for materials and information dealing with economic literacy in the K-12 environment. The site includes information on the NCEE network, teaching standards, programs, and a catalogue of publications.

EcEdWeb

http://ecedweb.unomaha.edu/

The pre-eminent clearinghouse for economic education in the U.S., EcEdWeb is a catalog of links for a wide variety of resources. The site is regularly maintained by Kim Sosin, co-director of the Center for Economic Education at the University of Nebraska-Omaha. The links are grouped under such headings as:

- Economics Resources for K-12 Teachers

- Economics Resources for College Teachers
- Links to Useful Economics Information and Data
- Links to Other Economic Education Sites

Most links include very informative, brief annotations. Don't miss the section "idea page on how to teach economics using the Internet" which is accessible from the pages for "Economics Resources for K-12 Teachers."

Friends & Partners Server: Economics & Business

http://www.friends-partners.org/friends/economics/
(Russian and English)
The Friends & Partners server is a large clearinghouse of information on a wide variety of topics related to Russia and the NIS. In particular, the "Economics & Business" section of the server has many good links. The site is subdivided into separate sections for publications and documents, business services, and economic/financial information. The "Publications" subsection is quite strong and provides the user with links to 10 different online sources, some of which are available in Russian language versions. These publications include "The New Generation," an electronic journal that features articles by economists, political scientists, and philosophers, and "Economics and Life," a publication which focuses on the Russian economy.

REESWeb: Russian and East European Studies

http://www.pitt.edu/~cjp/Econ/econgen.html
This site at the University of Pittsburgh offers an excellent annotated list of World Wide Web sites with information related to Russian and East European studies in the fields of business, economics, and law.

Resources for Economists on the Internet (EconFAQ)

http://wueconb.wustl.edu/EconFAQ/EconFAQ.html
Maintained by Bill Goffe of the Department of Economics at the University of Southern Mississippi, the EconFAQ is often cited as the most comprehensive list of links to Internet resources related to economics. The list is regularly maintained and includes hundreds of links. For each link Goffe provides a brief paragraph describing the site and sometimes offering some tips on how to navigate through it. When referencing a large site with many documents, Goffe will often create links to especially interesting documents.

Select List of Internet Resources for Teachers of Economics in Secondary Schools

http://www.ecom.unimelb.edu.au/ecowww/school.html

Although there are not a lot of links from this page, Robert Dixon, who compiled the list, seems to have a knack for finding good resources and good examples of how the Internet can be used for economic education. He also writes clear, useful annotations which highlight what the referenced site has to offer. Dixon is at the University of Melbourne and has links to a variety of Australian Web sites.

Syllabits

http://nsns.com/Syllabits/

Syllabits is a clearinghouse for course materials used in university-level business instruction and offers everything from lecture notes to actual homework assignments from courses taught in schools around the United States. There are specific sections for courses in accounting, economics, marketing, management, and finance. Citations appear in each section, giving the course name and level (i.e., undergraduate or graduate), as well as the professor's name and the name of the institution where the course was taught. Syllabits allows the user to link directly from the citation to the page where the information is held. Some of the links offer just basic course outlines and descriptions, but others give a great deal of information. The link to New York University's course on "Understanding World Macroeconomy" includes the course's reading list, homework assignments, and notes from all the lectures.

World Wide Resources in Economics (WebEc)

http://www.helsinki.fi/WebEc/

Another meta index to WWW resources in the field of economics, this one coming from Finland. WebEc is very easy to navigate.

Banking and Finance

Center for Banking Studies

University of North Carolina—Charlotte

http://www.uncc.edu/colleges/business/cbs/

This is a very interesting and useful banking Web site, based at the

University of North Carolina—Charlotte (UNCC). The site is a service of the University's Center for Banking Studies. The Center for Banking Studies is an academic organization within the Belk College of Business Administration at UNC—Charlotte. Banking and bank-related information is often difficult to locate on the Internet, so this site is especially valuable. Here are some of its contents:

- BankNet—contains World Wide Web links related to the business of banking—including bank sites on the Web, bank-related research available on the Web, and industry news posted on the Web.
- Banks on the Net—contains links to various national and international banks on the Net
- Banking & Finance Information Links—contains links to news and information sources relating to the banking community
- Banking & Finance Research and Statistics Links—contains links to various research resources relating to the banking community.
- Bank Regulatory Agencies—contains links to bank regulatory agencies.
- Banking Resource Centers—contains links to bank resource centers.

Business and Professional Associations

Association of Private Enterprise Education

http://www.utc.edu/~jclark/apee/

The mission of the Association of Private Enterprise Education is "to put into action accurate and objective understandings of private enterprise...Private enterprise is part and parcel of daily life for hundreds of millions of people in scores of nations around the world. Its abstract principles underlie economic, political, and social systems which allow unprecedented material affluence and broad personal freedoms. In democratic societies, however, private enterprise cannot be maintained without public understanding and support."

Specifically, the Association serves as an information exchange among those involved with private enterprise education, particularly in relation to research, teaching methods, programming, and sources of funding. It does so through yearly conferences, newsletters, membership directories, consultation among members, and other programs and publications. The overall theme of the 1998 annual conference, for example, was established as: "Economic Freedom of the World: Property Rights, Markets, and the Quality of Life." Papers accepted for presentation are eligible to be reviewed for publication in The Journal of Private Enterprise.

Individuals who share the Association's goals and represent schools, colleges and universities, businesses, government, foundations, labor unions, the media, or other institutions anywhere in the world are welcome to join the Association of Private Enterprise Education. Institutional memberships are also available. E-mail: jclark@utcvm.utc.edu

EconomicsAmerica Directory

http://www.economicsamerica.org/dir.html

A list of addresses and contact information for local and state affiliates of the National Council on Economic Education.

Foundation for Teaching Economics

http://www.fte.org/

Most of the site is information about FTE. It also contains the "National Standards in Economics," developed by the National Council on Economic Education. The document lists basic principles of a market economy, how it benefits society, and why students should study economics.

International Chamber of Commerce

http://www.iccwbo.org/

The ICC is a non-governmental organization whose members include thousands of businesses and business associations in more than 140 countries. ICC's main focus is on international trade. The ICC sponsors an International Court of Arbitration and has a Commercial Crime Services division which deal with maritime crime, fraud, and product counterfeiting.

International Ukrainian Economic Association

http://news.std.com/sabre/UFPWWW_Etc/Organizations/IUEA/IUEA.home.ht ml

The IUEA is an association of scholars interested in all aspects of Ukraine's economy. The site includes a description of the organization, the table of contents of the Association's annual journal, *Ukrainian Economic Review,* and a sample article, "External Shocks and Performance Responses during Systematic Transition: The Case of Ukraine."

National Association of Economic Educators

http://ecedweb.unomaha.edu/naee.htm

This association provides opportunities for the professional growth and recognition of its members through conferences, publications and awards. Learn how to become involved with it!

Union of International Associations

http://www.uia.org/homeorg.htm

This site offers links to hundreds of international organization Web sites based on a list compiled by the UIA. Many of them represent non-governmental organizations or professional associations.

United Kingdom Economics and Business Education Associations

http://bizednet.bris.ac.uk:8080/stafsup/subas.htm

A good list maintained at the Biz/ed Web site. (For more on this site, see page 15.)

U.S. Chamber of Commerce

http://www.uschamber.org/

The U.S. Chamber of Commerce is the world's largest business federation. The Chamber's Web site has information on its programs, including its programs abroad.

Businesses Online

EDGAR

http://www.sec.gov/edgarhp.htm

Maintained by the Securities and Exchange Commission, the U.S. government agency which regulates the stock market, EDGAR is an on-line database of financial reports that companies are required to submit to the government. Included are annual reports of most American corporations, and some foreign.

The Hall of Malls

http://nsns.com/MouseTracks/HallofMalls.html

Shopping malls which dot the American landscape have entered Cyberspace over the last couple of years. These malls offer a good opportunity to see the variety of businesses that exist in the U.S. and to see how they market their goods to the public. The Hall of Malls has links to hundreds of "virtual" malls, including places with names like "Buddha Town" and "The Capitalist Pig."

Hoover's

http://www.hoovers.com/

This site is intended primarily for investors; however, it has a number of features of use to students as well. The site includes a list of links to home pages of over 3,000 major American corporations. It also offers "Company Capsules" which include a brief description of what the company produces, its annual sales, and the number of employees.

Otis Index

http://www.otis.net/index.html

Another list of links to businesses which have a presence on the Internet. The Otis Index is organized by the kind of goods or services a business sells.

Consumers

American Council on Consumer Interests

http://acci.ps.missouri.edu

The mission of ACCI is "to provide a forum for the exchange of information about consumer issues and family economics to improve the well-being of individuals, households and families."

Consumer Information Catalog

http://www.pueblo.gsa.gov/catalog.htm

The U.S. government produces a large number of pamphlets and small booklets on issues which affect consumers. A good selection of these are available online from the government's Consumer Information Catalog. For example, listed under the "Money" section are brief booklets on such topics as: *Bankruptcy*, *Understanding Opportunities and Risks in Futures Trading*, and tips on how to invest wisely. The "Small Business" section includes brief guides which outline the steps needed to start and sell a business.

National Institute for Consumer Education

http://www.emich.edu/public/coe/nice/nice.html

Affiliated with the School of Education at Eastern Michigan University, NICE trains teachers, publishes education materials, and maintains a clearinghouse of teaching guides, pamphlets, and books. Its mission is to "to empower people to become informed consumers, reasoned decision makers, and participating citizens in a global marketplace." The primary audience is elementary and secondary school teachers. This site contains a large number of useful resources, including bibliographies for a variety of consumer issues and links to other consumer and personal finance Web sites. NICE also includes a series of mini-lesson plans on such topics as:

- College Student Budget
- Comparison Shopping
- Credit Issues: Women and Divorce
- Hang Up on Fraud
- How to Complain

Curriculum

Some of the documents described below are formatted in Adobe Acrobat™—an Internet utility which allows documents containing charts, tables and other graphics to move easily between a wide number of computer systems. In order to read documents featuring Adobe Acrobat you will need to install its "reader" on your computer. For instructions on how to do this, see "About Adobe Acrobat" in the appendix.

Most of these curricula are located at Web sites referenced elsewhere in this chapter. They are listed here individually to give a sense of the range of curricula that are currently available on the Internet. However, this is by no means a comprehensive list. If you are looking for curricula you should visit the other sites listed in this Guide, as they may have uploaded new materials since this document was compiled.

An Online Lesson on Demand

http://ecedweb.unomaha.edu/Dem_Sup/demand.htm

A draft of a lesson plan for teaching about demand by Kim Sosin of the EcEdWeb site at the University of Nebraska, Omaha. The lesson follows Bill who is about to enter college and has just been informed by his parents that he will be responsible for buying all his clothes. The lesson includes steps describing how students might use the Internet to investigate the price of blue jeans.

Economic Development Institute of the World Bank

http://www.worldbank.org/html/edi/home.html

This division of the World Bank focuses on international development and economies of states in transition. A major function of EDI is to provide teachers and trainers in these countries with resource materials relevant to the problems of economic development. Accessible from their Web site (under "Resources for Teachers and Trainers") is an index of case studies and training materials available, many in Russian. Materials cannot be accessed from the site, they must be ordered; however, detailed descriptions are given at the site. The case studies recount real life situations (for example, the problems encountered in privatizing a state-owned oil company in Russia) and describe how they were resolved. A listing of additional publications (such as research papers from World Bank projects) for ordering can also be found at this site.

Gang of 15

http://ecedweb.unomaha.edu/gang1.htm

A lesson about exchange rates in which students must track down an international gang of thieves and figure out how much they spent in different countries. For grades 4-10.

The Goat in the Rug

http://ecedweb.unomaha.edu/lit-goat.htm

A story for grades 1-3 which introduces the concepts of natural, human, and capital resources and intermediate goods.

Homer Price (The Doughnuts)

http://ecedweb.unomaha.edu/litdough.htm

A lesson plan for grades 4-6 which introduces the concepts of capital resources, increasing productivity, and the law of demand.

Principles of Macroeconomics

http://www.uakron.edu/econ/e201/e201rws.html

An online syllabus of a college economics course at the University of Akron. Of special interest are the homework assignments which provide ideas on Internet resources that can be used to fulfill the assignment.

Principles of Macroeconomics

http://www.colorado.edu/cewww/econ2020/

Another college level course, this time from the University of Colorado, this site is more than a syllabus but less extensive than a textbook. The course is divided into eight topics:

- The PPF and Comparative Advantage
- Demand, Supply, and Market Equilibrium
- Labor and Capital Markets, Inflation and Economic Growth
- Aggregate Demand, Supply, and Business Cycles
- Economic Thought and Keynesian Economics
- Money, Banking, and Monetary Policy
- International Trade and Finance
- Economic Growth and the Solow Growth Model

Each topic in turn consists of 10-15 sections which are 4-5 pages long and often include detailed discussions of complex economic concepts. Also included are homework assignments and links to Internet sites that can be used to complete the assignment.

Some Chapters Toward a Hypermedia Textbook for Principles of Economics

http://william-king.www.drexel.edu/top/classtuff.html

A professor of economics at Drexel University has begun to upload a textbook he is writing. Some of the chapters are already available. For the sections he hasn't finished, he has provided a syllabus for the college course he teaches.

Virtual Economics

http://ecedweb.unomaha.edu/ve.htm

Virtual Economics is the companion to a CD-ROM program of the same name which consists of lesson plans for economic education for grades K-12. Virtual Economics was produced by the National Council on Economic Education and the Nebraska Council on Economic Education. Located at this site are more than 30 downloadable lesson plans for elementary, middle level, and high school classes.

Economic Education

Business Education on the Internet: Biz/ed

http://bized.ac.uk

Biz/ed offers both a lot of content and links to useful business and economic education resources available on the Internet. Biz/ed is a non-profit consortium which includes Blackwell Publishers, the University of Bristol, and the Economics and Business Education Association, a professional association of British teachers of economics and business studies. Biz/ed also sponsors the *econ-business-educators* electronic mailing list.

The highlight is the section titled "Company Facts," which includes profiles of businesses. The profiles are presented in interview format in which a series of 15-20 questions are posed and answered.

The range of companies profiled includes:

- The Body Shop, a relatively small business which makes and sells cosmetics and toiletries
- The Financial Times
- Trades Union Congress, the major labor umbrella group in the UK
- British Petroleum

Among the challenging questions posed in the interviews are:

- What strategies does the business use in the process of quality control?
- What are some of the means used to motivate employees?
- What are examples of good employment practices?
- How is the business affected by government policy?
- Why do people join trade unions?
- How are trade unions financed?

- What is the role of trade unions in industrial disputes?
- What is the impact of trade unions on business?

Biz/ed International

http://bized.ac.uk/international

This is the international section of Business Education on the Internet and like Biz/ed, it also has an accompanying electronic mailing list. Biz/ed International "provides a gateway to the Internet for teachers and students of economics and business working in international schools. Its aim is to provide a whole range of quality resources that teachers and students will find useful in their classes." The e-mail list address is: int-econ-biz-educators@mailbase.ac.uk. Coordinator of Biz/ed International is Mark Waterson, whose e-mail address is: 106256.1712@compuserve.com.

Economics in the News

http://www.wwnorton.com/wsj/welcome.htm

A joint venture of W.W. Norton, a major publisher of textbooks, and *The Wall Street Journal*, America's largest newspaper, this site is for teachers who like to integrate today's headlines with their economic education curriculum. It is intended to be used in conjunction with three textbooks published by Norton: *Intermediate Microeconomics*, *Principles of Microeconomics*, and *Principles of Macroeconomics*. However, the site is also of interest to teachers who don't use these specific books.

For each book there is a collection of articles from *The Wall Street Journal* which illustrate key concepts used in the textbook. For example, in the section for *Intermediate Microeconomics* an article on a proposed tariff on the importation of silk products from China to the U.S. is used to explore the concept of "comparative advantage." At several places in the article the reader can click on hypertext links to brief documents which define economic concepts and pose questions, such as: "Does China have comparative advantage in the production of silk? How can this benefit other countries?"

Economics in the News is the brainchild of Hal Varian, dean of the School of Information Management and Systems and professor of economics at the University of California, Berkeley. Dr. Varian's home page (http://www.sims.berkeley.edu/~hal) has links to a variety of places on the Internet that are using Internet technology in new and intriguing ways.

Federal Reserve Board

http://www.bog.frb.fed.us/

The Federal Reserve Board is the central bank of the United States. The Fed and its 12 branch offices (http://www.bog.frb.fed.us/otherfrb.htm) are a major source of data about the U.S. economy. In addition to statistical data, each Fed office also publishes newsletters and analytical reports, many of which are available online. Perhaps most importantly, the Fed is a major source of online economic education materials, including:

The Federal Reserve System: Purposes and Functions

http://www.bog.frb.fed.us/pf/pf.htm

This is a large document available in Adobe Acrobat™ format which describes how the Fed works and to what ends. There are seven sections, each averaging around 200 kilobytes in size. The section on "Monetary Policy and the Economy" includes subsections on the goals of monetary policy, the effects of monetary policy on the economy, and the limitations of monetary policy.

Understanding the Home Mortgage Process

http://www.bog.frb.fed.us/pubs/mortgage/morbro_1.htm

This series of documents takes the reader through the steps of securing a home mortgage loan and provides information on what kinds of information lenders are looking for.

The Credit Process: A Guide for Small Business Owners

http://www.ny.frb.org/pihome/addpub/credit.html

This document outlines the steps owners of small business go though to apply for loans from banks. It includes explanations of what banks look at when considering loan applications.

U.S. Monetary Policy: An Introduction

http://www.frbsf.org/system/fedsystem/monpol/tofc.html

This is a short curriculum unit which includes a very good glossary of financial terms and a suggested reading list.

The Federal Reserve Bank of Minneapolis is an especially rich site for economic education materials. Through the home page (http://woodrow.mpls.frb.fed.us) the visitor will find a section on "Economic Education." Included here is "Teaching Economic Concepts Using the Internet," which includes four online class projects:

- Exchange Rates
- Savings
- Balancing the Federal Budget
- A Synthesis of Gross Domestic Product, Price Index, and Price Changes

Harvard Institute of Economic Research

http://www.economics.harvard.edu/hier/index.html

This site provides information on the current research work of professors in Harvard's economics department. A number of Harvard University's economists are involved in economic reform in the former Soviet states, and a surprising number of these were born there. The site offers an index of discussion and research papers published by Harvard economists from 1995 until the present. Examples include: "Paying the Bill for Goulash Communism," by Janos Kornai, and "Financial Crisis in Emerging Markets: The Lessons from 1995," by Jeffrey Sachs, Aaron Tornell, and Andres Velasco.

Currently, visitors to the site can view neither the text nor the abstract of a paper—just its title, author and date of publication. But there are instructions on how to order papers and soon all the papers, along with abstracts, will be available for downloading in Adobe Acrobat™ format directly from this Web site.

History of Economic Thought—McMaster University

http://socserv2.socsci.mcmaster.ca:80/~econ/ugcm/3ll3/index.html

As part of its History of Economic Thought class, McMaster University of Hamilton, Ontario has made available a "virtual library" of partial or complete works of influential economists. The site currently covers nearly 70 economists, including Jeremy Bentham, David Hume, Thomas Malthus, Alfred Marshall, Karl Marx, John Stuart Mill, Vilfredo Pareto, David Ricardo, Adam Smith, and Thorstein Veblen, among others. Works include Marshall's *The Principles of Economics*, Marx's *Capita*l (Vol. I), Malthus' *An Essay on the Principle of Population*, J.S. Mill's *Principles of Political Economy*, Veblen's *Theory of the Leisure Class*, and Smith's *Wealth of Nations*. It is unclear exactly how many of the works in this archive are complete texts; even with that caveat, this is an extraordinary introduction to the history of economic thought. These texts are in ASCII format for easy downloading and reading, but many are very large files.

Journal of Economic Education

http://www.indiana.edu/~econed/

The *Journal of Economic Education* is a professional journal which carries articles on innovations in teaching economics. This site does not contain the journal articles but it does have a well-organized, searchable database of article abstracts.

McEachern Economics

http://www.thomson.com/swcp/bef/mceachern/mceachern.html

Another example of using the Internet to supplement a textbook, this site is sponsored by South-Western College Publishing, which produces three textbooks: a general introduction to economics and two others on microeconomics and macroeconomics, respectively. For each textbook the website contains a table of contents with chapters and sub-chapter headings. Each heading has a link to a "teachers guide," which includes Internet sites that can be incorporated into the teaching cirriculum, plus some suggested classroom exercises and questions. For example, the general introduction to economics textbook includes a section titled "The Economic Actors: Households, Firms, Governments, and the Rest of the World." The associated Internet resources section for this chapter include links to Toyota (a Japanese car manufacturer) and a "virtual" law firm. There are 140 different Internet sites referenced for the general economics textbook.

National Center for Research in Economic Education

http://www.cba.unl.edu/additional/econed/ncree.html

The Center conducts research, evaluates programs, and conducts surveys. The Center has developed a series of tests to measure the economic literacy of students in elementary and high school. This site is home to the Center's Research in Economic Education Database (REED), which contains abstracts of over 1,000 journal articles on research in economic education. The database is categorized by grade level and topic.

Economic News and Analysis

All of the world's major financial publications, e.g. *The Wall Street Journal*, *The Financial Times*, now have online editions. Some also provide excellent resources for high school teachers or college teachers. If you are not already familiar with these services, the sites below will lead you to many of the best.

Central Europe Online

http://www.centraleurope.com/

Central Europe Online is an online daily newspaper which is targeted primarily at Western businesses interested in expanding to Eastern Europe. Each issue carries the day's important political and business news, plus some feature stories. Some of the stories are abstracts of longer articles that are available to business subscribers, but they are interesting nonetheless.

EAST

http://www.ssc.upenn.edu/east/index.html

EAST is the quarterly newsletter of the Economies and Societies in Transition Center at the University of Pennsylvania which focuses on Eastern Europe and the former USSR. Each issue includes three or four scholarly articles. As of October 1996 only three issues had been uploaded, but more are expected.

The Economist

http://www.enews.com/magazines/economist/

Read in over 180 countries, *The Economist* is one of the most respected English language newsmagazines in the world. Among the many publications hosted at The Electronic Newsstand (see below), The Economist Web site includes the table of contents and a few articles from the current issue. Select articles from past issues are also available. Every two to three weeks, *The Economist* includes a special 15-20 page section, or "Survey," which focuses on a particular topic. In the past year, these Surveys have focused on topics such as:

- A Survey of International Banking: The Domino Effect
- The Survey of Central Europe
- A Survey of Multinationals: Big is Back
- A Survey of Russia's Emerging Market

The Electronic Newsstand usually includes the lead article from these special surveys.

The Electronic Newsstand

http://www.enews.com

The Electronic Newsstand 'hosts' over 200 magazines and includes links to more than 2,000 newspaper and magazine Web sites. Typically, 'hosting' means that the Newsstand includes the cover, table of contents, and a few articles of a magazine's current issue. For many publications, the Newsstand also has a searchable archive of select back articles. There are a number of major business magazines available through the Newsstand.

RAND

http://www.rand.org/organization/nsrd/russ.economy/

This site is dedicated to an analysis of Russia's informal economy. It is a relatively new site and will develop as material on this topic becomes available.

Russia Today

http://www.russiatoday.com/

Brought to you by the same people who publish *Central Europe Online, Russia Today* is an online newspaper targeted primarily at Western businesses operating in Russia or thinking of investing there. It carries political and economic news with three or four feature articles per issue.

Government and Other Sources of Economic Data

Bank of Finland

Unit for Eastern European Economies

http://www.bof.fi/env/eng/it/iten.stm

Due to the long-standing political and commercial significance of Russia and Eastern Europe to Finland, the Bank of Finland (the nation's central bank) maintains a unique research resource dedicated to the study of these economies in transition. It is the Unit for Eastern European Economies and much of its work is available at its Web site. The unit's primary mission is to monitor and provide economic analysis of developments in economies in transition, particularly Russia and the Baltic states.

As part of a central bank organization, the unit enjoys access to an exceptionally diverse range of international databases and other information sources. Through these resources, the unit provides a central banking perspective in its analysis of subjects such as monetary stabilization, development of financial systems, and international integration.

Among the unit's regular publications is *Russian and Baltic Economies—The Week in Review.* This is a weekly news summary in electronic format focusing on events affecting economic development in Russia, the Baltics and other transition economies. It is available by e-mail or fax delivery every Friday. To be added to the mailing list for "*Russian and Baltic Economies—The Week in Review*" contact Timo Harell (timo.harell@bof.fi)

Once a year the bank's Unit for East European Economies also publishes a compilation of its main analyses and articles as a book. Publications are provided free of charge in most cases. Following are the URL's for the most useful sections of the bank's Web site, all in English.

- Review of Economies in Transition
  http://www.bof.fi/env/eng/it/enlista/enbase.stm

- Russian and Baltic Economies—The Week in Review
  http://www.bof.fi/env/eng/it/weekly/weekbase.stm

- Books. A collection of articles in English and Finnish containing studies and surveys
  http://www.bof.fi/env/eng/it/booklist/booklist.stm

- Core research team
  http://www.bof.fi/env/eng/it/itorg/itenorg.stm

Bureau of Labor Statistics

http://stats.bls.gov/blshome.html

The Bureau of Labor Statistics (BLS) is one of the U.S. federal government's major producers of statistics about the U.S. economy. It maintains data on a variety of economic indicators, including unemployment, wage and price levels, and productivity. BLS also includes a special section for international data (http://stats.bls.gov/flshome.htm). This site is home to *How the Government Measures Unemployment* (http://stats.bls.gov/cps_htgm.htm), a document which defines "unemployment," describes how unemployment statistics are collected, and analyzes issues such as "seasonal employment."

Business Information Service for the Newly Independent States (BISNIS)

http://www.iep.doc.gov/bisnis/bisnis.html

BISNIS is a project of the US Government's Department of Commerce. It describes its Web site as a "one-stop shop for doing business in Russia and the other states of the former Soviet Union." The site is in English and is obviously geared towards the American business person or investor interested in Russia/NIS; however, there is valuable economic information to be found here. The site contains reports on the economic well-being of the various states of the NIS, such as an overview of Ukraine's trade and investment environment. The site's Ukraine section also contains a "country commercial guide," that explains in detail the post-Soviet development and current state of Ukraine's economic policies. Additionally, the site features reports on different industry sectors (e.g. energy, agribusiness, consumer goods) in the NIS. This industry section contains a searchable database.

The BISNIS Web site contains an entire section devoted to "other sources"—an index of different sites relevant to the NIS. The majority of links in the section are related to either Russia or US Government sites that contain information on Russia/NIS (e.g. the US Trade & Development Agency). Most of the Russian sites mentioned in this section are commercial in nature and deal with business and banking services in Russia.

Census Bureau

http://www.census.gov/

The U.S. Census Bureau Web site offers much more than just how many people live in the U.S. (See, for example, *Eurasia Bulletin* below.) The data available includes information on where Americans live, how they get to work, what they do at work, where they buy their groceries, and much, much more. The Web site also has a section titled "Just for Fun," which is intended for young students.

CIA

http://www.odci.gov/cia/publications/pubs.html

The Central Intelligence Agency publishes an annual *World Factbook* and puts it up on the Web. It is one of the best places on the Internet to get basic information on 268 countries, territories, city-states, and islands. For each country the *Factbook* includes information on natural resources, population and demographics, geography, government and political information, and a whole host of statistics on the economy and industrial production. The CIA's *Handbook of International Economic Statistics* provides basic worldwide statistics which can be used to compare the economic performance of major countries and regions. The 1995 edition includes a special section on the former USSR. The *Factbook* also features many nice charts and tables of economic data, some of which are over 100 KB in size.

Econon Data & Links

http://www.csufresno.edu/Economics/econ_EDL.htm
This page is maintained by John Shaw of the California State University in Fresno because, in his words, "Over the years I have found that I cannot always remember the current value of a particular economic statistic." Shaw has created a table which shows basic economic data for the U.S., including population, income distribution, productivity, interest rates, etc. What makes the page interesting is that in addition to providing the current numbers, he also has created links to the sites where he found the data.

Eurasia Bulletin

http://www.census.gov/ipc/www/eb.html
The International Programs Center (IPC), part of the Population Division of the U.S. Bureau of the Census, conducts demographic and socioeconomic studies and strengthens statistical development around the world through technical assistance, training, and software products. Its work is commissioned and funded by federal agencies, international organizations, non-governmental organizations, private businesses, and other governments.
For over 50 years IPC has assisted in the collection, processing, analysis, dissemination, and use of statistics with counterpart governments throughout the world.

The International Programs Center publishes "Eurasia Bulletin," an interesting newsletter that is not widely known. Recent issues included the following discussions:

- Standard of Living in Ukraine
- Profile of Donetsk (Ukraine)
- Demographic Developments in Eastern Europe and the former Soviet Union: Present and Future
- Pension Reform in China: Preparing for the Future

The Bulletin is also available electronically on the Bureau of the Census Web site. Documents can be downloaded in html and/or Acrobat pdf format. For more information, e-mail: ipc@census.gov

European Union

http://europa.eu.int

This is the home page of the European Commission, the governing body of the European Union. From here you can find data about the EU including information on its political and economic institutions. The site also includes links to other EU institutions and to government sites of EU members.

International Monetary Fund

http://www.imf.org

This site contains news briefs, press releases, meeting information, the full text of certain IMF publications, and more. An especially useful part of the site is a directory of international economic, commodity, and development organizations, with a brief but informative overview of the organization plus contact information (http://www.imf.org/external/np/sec/decdo/contents.htm).

Japan's Assistance to the Newly Independent States

http://www.infoweb.or.jp/scc/

(in Russian, English, and Japanese)

Japan has actively participated in the reform processes of the former Soviet states and provided extensive economic assistance since 1991. This page details the projects Japan has implemented throughout the NIS, including Ukraine. The majority of materials available on this Web site are descriptions of Japanese-funded projects, such as the Regional Venture Fund, which provides assistance to small businesses in the NIS. The page also contains a detailed outline (under the "List of Commitments" section) of monies dispersed to different NIS states since 1991.

OECD/CCET

http://www.oecd.org/sge/ccet/

The Organization for Economic Co-operation and Development (OECD) was founded in 1961 as heir to the international organization which administered the Marshall Plan in Europe after World War II. The OECD's Centre for Co-operation with the Economies in Transition (CCET) was established in 1990 to provide assistance to Eastern Europe, the NIS, Mongolia, and Vietnam as these countries seek to create pluralist democracies and market economies.

In addition to general information about CCET's programs and print publications, this site also contains CCET's reports and economic surveys of Hungary, Poland, the Slovak Republic, and Russia, for example. Some of the reports are a couple of years old but they have interesting charts and tables of figures. The site also contains an electronic version of the CCET's quarterly newsletter, *Transition in Brief.* Each issue includes a couple of feature articles, such as "New survey assesses growth prospects" and "Assisting the development of capital markets;" case studies; a calendar of upcoming events; and reviews of new books and publications about the process of economic transition in the region.

Penn World Data

http://bizednet.bris.ac.uk:8080/dataserv/pennhome.htm

Penn World Data is a dataset which includes statistics covering 28 key economic variables for all of the world's major economies from 1960 to the early 1990s. The data itself is located at the National Bureau of Economic Research at Harvard University (http://nber/harvard.edu). However, the Biz/ed WWW site contains a good overall description of how to format and submit searches of the Penn World Data dataset. It also provides an example of how one would conduct a search in order to test a theory (e.g., is the level of real income directly related to the level of investment?).

Statistical Agencies

http://www.ssb.no/www-open/english/web_servers/

For people who never have enough numbers, this site is a list of links to organizations (often governments) all over the world which keep track of statistics.

Statistical Agencies on the Internet

http://www.science.gmu.edu/csi779/drope/govstats.html

Another list of (mostly national) statistical agencies that have Internet sites. This directory provides not only the agencies home page but also the place within the Web site which contains data—a needed service for some Web sites which are so big it's difficult to find what you want.

UK Office for National Statistics

http://bizednet.bris.ac.uk:8080/dataserv/csohome.htm

18 datasets of economic, financial, and social data for the U.K. is available through an easy-to-use form provided by Biz/ed.

United Nations Development Programme

Regional Bureau for Europe and the CIS

http://www.undp.org/undp/rbec/

The United Nations Development Programme's Regional Bureau for Europe and the CIS (UNDP/RBEC) publishes a report annually, titled "Human Development Under Transition: Europe and CIS." It is a compendium of 25 National Human Development Reports and describes human development trends in countries of Central and Eastern Europe, the Baltic States and the CIS (Commonwealth of Independent States). It can be found online at RBEC's Web site along with the full text of the National Human Development Reports for each of the countries in the region (listed below), as well as other publications and information on UNDP/RBEC's activities in the region. The compendium covers areas such as governance, the economy, poverty, social trends, gender considerations and human settlements. Additional features include a series of maps of each country and special sections devoted to other recent RBEC publications on gender, human settlements and poverty.

The countries covered in the publication are: Albania, Armenia, Azerbaijan, Belarus, Bulgaria, Czech Republic, Estonia, Georgia, Hungary, Kazakhstan, Kyrgyz Republic, Latvia, Lithuania, Malta, Moldova, Poland, Romania, Russian Federation, Slovak Republic, Tajikistan, Turkey, Turkmenistan, Ukraine, Uzbekistan and Yugoslavia.

The World Bank

http://www.worldbank.org/

The World Bank's Web site is a treasure-trove of information. Among the many highlights are the complete texts of select World Bank research reports, such as:

- Bureaucrats in Business: The Economics and Politics of Government Ownership
- Emerging Stock Markets Factbook 1996
- Global Economic Prospects and the Developing Countries 1996
- The Plundering of Agriculture in Developing Countries
- Toward Gender Equality. The Role of Public Policy

The Bank's online publications catalog can be accessed via the "Publications" section and offers the following:

- Up-to-date information on Bank publications
- Full text summaries of major Bank publications, including:
  - ✓ World Development Report
  - ✓ Global Economic Prospects
  - ✓ Bureaucrats in Business
  - ✓ Emerging Stockmarkets Factbook
- A full-text feature article from each issue of:
  - ✓ Financial Flows and the Developing Countries
  - ✓ Commodity Markets and the Developing Countries
- Table of contents and article abstracts for:
  - ✓ The World Bank Economic Review
  - ✓ The World Bank Research Observer
  - ✓ Finance and Development
- Reviews of Bank publications from professional journals
- Data samples from Bank statistical products

This site also contains numerous sets of economic data; however, for some the search directions may be a little confusing. There is also a section containing analytical economics articles (http://www.worldbank.org/html/prdmg/grthweb/datasets.htm).

Too Much Data? Would You Like to Hear a Joke or Two?

As an economic educator you want to learn about the best the Internet has to offer for your work. But by now you may be experiencing mild symptoms of information overload. Here are two sites that have jokes by, for, and about economists, proving that even members of "the dismal science" have a sense of humor.

- http://quasar.csuchico.edu/econ/links/econhumor.html
- http://netec.wustl.edu/JokEc.html

Interactive Games

Be Your Own Chancellor!

http://www.ifs.org.uk/byoc97/byoc97_in.htm

Be Your Own Chancellor is an online computer model which enables visitors to see how different tax rates will affect various socio-economic categories of citizens in Britain. (Chancellor of the Exchequer is the title of the minister of the treasury or finance in Great Britain.) The game uses nine families: some married, some not; some unemployed; some with one wage earner, some with two; and a retired couple. For each family there is a budget based on how much the family earns and spends on basic consumer items like rent, food, savings, etc. Using the computer, model you can see what effect the income tax rate will have on each of the families. You can also adjust tax deducations for mortages, have different tax allowances, change taxes on consumer goods, etc. The model is part of a World Wide Web site maintained by the Institute of Fiscal Studies (http://www1.ifs.org.uk), a think tank in London. The Institute's Web site also includes abstracts and publications by IFS researchers on a wide variety of British budget and tax issues.

Currency Comparison Project

http://www.wimmera.net.au/CurrComp/CurrComp.html

An example of the way the Internet can be integrated into a course on economics, the Currency Conversion Project was created at a K-12 school in Hirsham, Australia. The project uses Coca-Cola and Big Mac hamburgers to help students understand concepts of nominal and real exchange rates. Visitors are told how many liters of Coca-Cola and hamburgers $5 Australian will buy. Then they are asked to convert (currency converter provided) the $5 into their own currency and asked how many Cokes and burgers they could buy with that amount. Responses around the world are available so that students can compare relative purchasing power.[1]

---

[1] The site in Australia might not always have the most up-to-date exchange rates or rates for some of the smaller countries. Please see Appendix D, "Finding Exchange Rates and Share Prices," for Internet sites offering more complete exchange rate information.

EduStock

http://tqd.advanced.org/3088

This site contains the clearest, most straightforward explanation of the Stock Market we found on the Web, including a very helpful glossary. It also is host to a Stock Market simulation game. However, what is really impressive is that this site was prepared by three high school students as a summer project!

The Stock Market Game

http://www.smg2000.org/

The Stock Market Game is an electronic simulation of Wall Street trading, providing students with an understanding of the stock market, the sources and uses of capital, and other economic concepts. Established in 1977, the game is played by teams (usually three to five students) in grades 4-12, who make an initial investment of (a hypothetical) $100,000 in stocks listed on the American Stock Exchange, the New York Stock Exchange, and NASDAQ (the exchange for "over the counter" securities). For ten weeks teams buy and sell stock, pay commissions, and try to increase the value of their portfolio.

The Stock Market Game is sponsored nationally by the Securities Industry Foundation for Economic Education, whose goal is to "foster among the public a better understanding of both the American economic system and the role of the securities industry within that system." It is managed at the state level by affiliates of the National Council on Economic Education. Sometimes newspapers and businesses also participate in the project. In Chicago, for instance, *The Chicago Tribune* contributes newspapers to each class and prepares a guide for how to read the investment section of the paper. Local brokers will often provide technical support.

Links to other stock market simulations, targeted primarily for investors, can be found at Yahoo at:

http://www.yahoo.com/Recreation/Games/Gambling/Interactive_Web_Games/Stock_Market/

Labor

AFL-CIO

http://www.aflcio.org/index.htm

The AFL-CIO is a coordinating/umbrella organization for most of America's major labor unions. Its approximately 80 member unions represent over 13 million American workers. The AFL-CIO provides technical assistance to workers who wish to start unions at their place of work. It also advocates on behalf of workers to the U.S. Congress and other branches of the state and federal government. The AFL-CIO Web site includes policy statements and press releases which articulate labor's perspective on current events and legislation. The site also includes a list of links to Web sites of many American labor unions.

History of U.S. Labor

http://www.kentlaw.edu/ilhs/curriculum.html

The history of the labor movement in the U.S. is among the more dramatic and conflictual of all industrialized nations. Prepared by the Illinois Labor History Society, this is a curriculum, complete with classroom handouts, for teaching about the history of the U.S. labor movement. The curriculum traces labor from the colonial period, when many people came to the U.S. as indentured servants or slaves, to the present. A guiding theme of the curriculum is to show how "laborers have earned a voice in the workplace and increased their share of the economic pie."

Industrial and Labor Relations

http://www.ilr.cornell.edu/

Cornell University's School of Industrial and Labor Relations has a Web site which serves as a good catalog to Internet resources relating to the academic study of labor and the workplace relationship between employer and employee. It includes online versions of several government task force reports covering such topics as the "glass ceiling" for women and labor and management relations in local and state governments.

Labor Link

http://laborlink.simplenet.com/

A list of links to labor organizations, Web sites with information related to unions and labor issues, and online articles and texts about labor.

Russian Sites

The following sites are in Russian only, unless otherwise indicated. In order to read documents at these sites, your computer must have Cyrillic fonts installed.

Central Bank of the Russian Federation

http://www.cbr.ru/

This site is packed with information on Russia's official banking and monetary structure. If you need information on currency reform or governmental attempts to combat inflation in Russia, this is the place to go. The site provides a search mechanism so that users may do a keyword search to find information. The site is divided into sections in the form of long articles that appear to be updated frequently. Topics covered include:

- Currency
- The banking system
- The history of the bank

Additionally, there are sections devoted to statistics which include information on the balance of payments from 1995 to the present, the bank's gold reserves, and fluctuations in the ruble. This site maintains a database which can access the exchange rate of any international currency versus the ruble on any given day since 1 January 1996. Furthermore, there is a list of publications issued by the Central Bank (mostly in Russian) and an index of bank press releases.

The Economic Development Institute of the World Bank, Moscow Office (EDIMO)

Всемирный Банк Институт Экономического Развития , Мовсковское Представительство

http://www.edimo.ru/Web.htm

(Russian and English)

The Economic Development Institute Moscow Office focuses on economic education and training for government employees and economic educators. This site contains several sections, including:

- Macroeconomic policy and management
- Privatization and the development of the private sector
- Analysis of investment projects and their implementation
- Social policy and the development of human resources

While much of the information on this Web site concerns the courses and programs offered by EDIMO, there are several "forums" that provide in-depth discussion and analysis of various economic themes. These include:

- "Economic growth in the countries of Southeast Asia"
- "The restructuring of enterprises in the countries of the former USSR"
- "Unemployment and the labor market in Central and Eastern Europe"
- "Unemployment in Russia 1992—1996: Its growth, characteristics, and regional variations"
- "Issues of poverty and social politics in Russia"

Of particular interest is EDIMO's Department of Macroeconomic Policy (http://www.edimo.ru/EDIMP/edimp.htm), which applies the experience of the World Bank to help train government employees and economic educators in the basics of market economics and macroeconomic policy. In cooperation with various educational institutes, including Moscow State University, the Economic University of Uzbekistan, and the Academy of Government Service in Ukraine, the Department of Macroeconomic Policy has established training facilities throughout the former Soviet Union. The Department's Web page contains an interesting forum on "Economic Policy Issues in Transition." This forum covers such topics as:

- Liberalization of trade and the politics of stimulating exports
- Reduction of the budget deficit and management of the public debt
- Analysis and management of government expenditures
- Stimulating economic growth

Additonally, EDIMO's Department of Macroeconomic Policy Web page contains a section on "interactive programs for long distance learning." There is also an English language site at http://www.edimo.ru/Web_e.htm (although it contains less information) than the Russian site, and links to the World Bank home page.

Emerging Markets Navigator

http://feast.fe.msk.ru/koi/infomarket/emn/

The EMN World Wide Web site was established in August 1995 to provide access to information about financial markets in the former USSR. It is the as a home for a couple of independent companies: Skate Press, which publishes *Capital Markets Russia*, a weekly newsletter, and sells financial information online; and the Rating Information Center (RIC), which provides financial information on many of Russia's major banks. RIC has published online the credit rating of Moscow banks for the period of November 1995—January 1996.

Federal Commission for the Securities Market

http://www.fe.msk.ru/win/infomarket/fedcom/ewelcome.html
(Russian and English)
This agency is responsible for supervising the development of the Russian Federation's capital market, ensuring the protection of investors' rights, and maintaint the legal opperation of the capital and securities market. The commission's Web site is accordingly filled with official documents on market regulations and rules, government decrees, and recently passed legislation from the Russian parliament. The "What's New" section gives a chronological listing of the latest news events relevant to Russian securities and is updated frequently. Examples of news items in this section include a feature story on negotiations between Russia's Central Bank, the FCSM, and First Deputy Anatoly Chubais on new market regulations, and a listing of new agreements between the FCSM and the St. Petersburg local government. The site also contains several links to relevant sources, including Infomarket—a commercial service that provides daily updates on the Russian security exchange.

Higher School of Economics Institute of Macroeconomic Research and Forecasting (IMRF)

http://www.ru/imrf/PAGE/imrf.htm (Russian)
http://www.ru/imrf/index.htm (English)
(Russian and English)
IMRF is a service which provides forecasts for a fee, but the site has free three-month forecasts on 11 macroeconomic indicators. The forecasts include a review of trends over the past three years with IMRF's forecast for the next three months. Forecast graphs include:

- Real average per capita monthly incomes
- Average monthly wage
- Consumer price index
- Producer price index
- Retail sales volume
- Imports and exports
- Number of registered jobless
- Index of industrial production
- Construction statistics

InfoArt Server

http://www.infoart.ru/mainmenu.htm

InfoArt is an Internet-based news service and offers an extensive array of publications and news items for online perusal. The site contains everything from the schedule of the Bolshoi Theatre to the latest issue of *Computer Week* magazine. The server is updated daily and its "Business and Finance" section includes news from Interfax, *Argumenti i Fakti*, and Finmarket, among others. In addition to news articles, this site also contains the latest figures from international stock exchanges and markets, commercial bank ratings, and currency exchanges. While the site's main menu can be overwhelming—the sheer volume of information combined with flashing advertisements can confuse the user—but with some patience this site will yield extensive resources related to economic education.

The Institute for the Economy in Transition

http://www.online.ru/sp/

The Institute for Economy in Transition is an organization led by Yegor Gaidar. The site has a section on "Russian Economic Tendencies and Perspectives" which includes articles on alternative economic policies, problems of inflation and macroeconomic stabilization, and the organization's monthly bulletin, *Russian Economics: Tendencies and Perspectives*. Back issues of the bulletin contain some useful charts and graphs on various aspects of the Russian economy, including numbers for the execution of the Russian budget, the deficit of the federal budget, indicators of financial markets, and the dynamics of basic macroeconomic indexes.

Moscow "Business World" Bank

http://www.mdm.ru/default.htm

(Russian and English)

The majority of the materials contained at the site deal with promoting the bank and its services; however, the "online services" section provides current quotes from the Russian financial markets (e.g. money market funds, treasury bills, etc.). Several of these quote sections are still under construction, but the section featuring exchange rates for NIS currencies versus the dollar is functioning and is updated daily.

Moscow Libertarium

http://www.fe.msk.ru/libertarium/ehomepage.html

(Russian and English)

The Moscow Libertarium is a project dedicated to the "support of social activity and scientific research on the problems of liberalism," or what is known in the United States as "libertarianism." Libertarians favor small government and a minimum of laws and regulation. The site contains a number of in-depth articles on economic issues written from a libertarian perspective. Libertarium project members have translated several articles into English, but the selection of materials in Russian is much greater. A few of the articles available at the site are: "Liberalism, Customary Rights, and Economic Reforms," by Vitaly Naishul and "Conservative Liberalism in Modern Russia." The site also provides a large index of Web-links related to international libertarianism and "classical liberal" thought.

Moscow State University of Economics, Statistics & Computer Science (MESI)

http://www.mesi.ru/web/homerus.htm

The MESI home page is mainly devoted to describing the structure of the university's departments and programs. It lacks much data or links to other valuable sites. However, there is a useful section that lists upcoming conferences and symposia related to economics and computer science in the Moscow area, along with contact names and addresses.

Nizhny Novgorod Region Administration Department of Economics and Forecasting

Департамент Экономики и Прогнозирования

http://www.kreml.nnov.ru/

This is the home page for the Economics Department of Nizhny Novgorod, one of the most economically successful regions of the Russian Federation. While much of the information is specific to the Nizhny Novgorod oblast, this site also contains a wealth of information on the economic transformation of the country as a whole.

Of specific interest is the "Review of the macroeconomic situation in the Nizhny Novgorod oblast and Russia 1991—1996." In addition to a broad overview of the "Transition from a socialist to a world economy," this section offers a comprehensive but easily understandable economic synopsis of each year, providing an analysis of policy and a forecast of future trends. The use of diagrams and charts to illustrate points in this section is very good.

Other topics on this Web site include:

- "A survey of the financial sector of the Nizhny Novgorod oblast," analyzing the local financial and stock markets.
- "Information on the execution of various programs in the Nizhny Novgorod oblast," which contains information on both local and federal programs in the region during 1994-1996. The information is displayed in both a table summary and in more detailed text format, which covers specific sectors, such as ecology, social assistance, infrastructure, and agriculture.
- Information on the investment climate and investment opportunities in the Nizhny Novgorod region, including a listing of over 600 projects.
- A database of 110 economic indicators compiled on January 1, 1997. A demonstration version of this database can be downloaded.

Additionally, this Web page contains links to many other interesting sites. These include:

- Two databases of Federal and regional legislation
- References to "the most interesting free Web sites on economic themes"
- Links to government servers for the countries of the NIS, including the Moscow city government, the Russian Federation, the Federal Securities Commission, and the Parliament of Georgia.

Relis Online

http://www.relis.ru

This site is sponsored by Relcom, one of Russia's largest Internet service providers. Relis is a news and information service and its Web site contains a lot of material related to economics and finance. One can access the latest figures from the Russian stock exchanges and commodities markets in the "biznis" section. For example, you can easily find information on diamond trading on the Russian exchange. The "info-agencies" section contains short analytical reviews of Russian political and economic life from various information services, and includes the latest news from Russian radio.

There are also several online versions of popular Russian newspapers at the site, including *Russkaia Mysl, Literaturnaia Gazeta, Izvestia Finansovye* and *Izvestia.* The latter two require the user to subscribe (and pay) in order to view the past issues, but the latest issue can be freely accessed. The remaining papers can all be accessed without a fee, including past issues.

Russia-online Business and Finance

Россия-он-лайн Бизнес и Финансы

http://www.online.ru/rmain/rbiz

(Russian and English)

Russia-online is a server which contains a wealth of links to other Internet sites. The main Web page (http://www.online.ru/) covers not only economics, but a variety of topics on the Russian Federation, including news, online magazines, sports, legal and cultural affairs, travel, and even weather. The Russia-online Business and Finance section has links to both free and fee-based sites, although the majority of references are to free sources. Some of the sites referenced are in English; however the overwhelming majority are in Russian.

Of particular interest are the news sources, which contain links to online magazines and ClariNet newsgroups. One particularly interesting magazine, *Expert* (*Эксперт*, http://www.expert.ru/), contains in-depth articles on investment, regional economies, the stock market, and an archive of previous issues. The Business and Finance site also has links to Dun & Bradstreet's "Guide to the Russian Stock Market;" however, this document is available only in English.

Additionally, the Business and Finance page contains links to Russian and English language sources, most of them commercial, on topics such as:

- Banking & finance, which has links to banks throughout the Russian Federation, including the Central Bank
- Business schools, both Russian and foreign
- Investing and the stock market, which contains stock quotes and information on mutual funds
- The labor market, including job hunting sources

Russia-online is also the server for the Institute for the Economy in Transition, Yegor Gaidar's think tank, and the Russia-online Business and Finance page has links to current and past issues of the Institute's newsletter "Russian Economics: Tendencies and Perspectives."

Russian Commission for the Securities Market

http://www.fe.msk.ru/infomarket/fedcom/ewelcome.html

Established in July 1996, the Federal Commission for the Securities Market is a ministerial-level government agency with a mandate to supervise the development of Russia's capital market. The site contains news releases about the Commission's actions and some official Commission documents.

Russian Federation Chamber of Commerce & Industry

http://www.rbcnet.ru/

(Russian and English)

The purpose of a chamber of commerce is to support businesses and promote economic growth in a given region. The Russian Federation's Chamber of Commerce is no different—thus, this site is dedicated to the promotion of Russian business ventures and Russian industries. A large part of the materials available here simply advertise different projects and ventures—the "news" section, for example, consists of advertisements of ventures and solicitations for business partners. However, the "Analytical Research" section contains lengthy articles on such topics as the development of Russian tax codes or the insurance market. The site also contains a search mechanism that allows the user to look for materials at the site using a keyword search. Although the index and main page of this site are in English, almost all other aspects (articles, news items, etc.) are only in Russian.

St. Petersburg Stock Exchange

http://bsd.lse.spb.su/

(Russian and English)

An exhaustive amount of data related to the St. Petersburg Stock Exchange can be found at this site: the history of the exchange, daily trading figures, plus some very complicated databases that actually plot graphs illustrating activity in the municipal and federal bond markets! Additionally, there are links to the economic journal "New East," the ITAR-TASS news agency's online service, and CNN's online financial news service—but the majority of information here is data from the exchange. You can also link from here to the Siberian Stock Exchange.

Siberian Stock Exchange

http://www.sse.nsk.su/

The Web page of the Siberian Stock Exchange contains only a small percentage of the facts and figures available on the St. Petersburg Stock Exchange site. For the most part, it is limited to a discussion of stock exchange's history and structure. It also maintains a list of contact names, addresses, and phone numbers.

Uchitelskaya Gazeta

http://www.ug.ru/

This site is the online archive for the respected weekly publication, *Uchitelskaya Gazeta* (Teacher's Magazine). Each issue includes stories on present problems for educators, educational projects for the classroom, learning games, and other suggestions for teachers. There are also sections dedicated to specific subjects such as sports, English, and geography.

Women in Business—Russia

Женщины в Бизнесе-Россия

http://www.cbi.co.ru/wib

This site is hosted by the Business Collaboration Center, a project sponsored by the U.S. Agency for International Development (http://www.info.usaid.gov) and administered by the Citizens Democracy Corps (http://www.cdc.org). It includes a large number of pointers to other sites and sources of information regarding business development in Russia. According to Women in Business (WIB), "Women in Russia are well-suited for entrepreneurial ventures and small business operation. The practical and invaluable training of running a household while working full time and caring for multiple generations of family has helped Russian women to develop essential entrepreneurial skills: flexibility, adaptation, perseverance, creativity, resourcefulness, balancing of budgets, etc.

Elements of the Women in Business—Russia web site include individual Web pages profiling the many different business organizations throughout the country. WIB will develop a business's Web page and upload it to their site at no cost. Another element of the Women in Business web site is a review of news items from different women's business organizations.

There are also plans to establish a listserv to provide an open forum for women in business to share thoughts, ideas, questions, etc. To participate, send an e-mail to Marina Matveeva at BCC (wib@bcc.ru) and attach text files with information about your organization (ideally in both English and Russian, although either one will do), a computer file of your logo and computer files with anything else you want to include. You can also send suggestions on other elements to add to the Web page to Ms. Matveeva.

Schools Online

EdWeb

http://edweb.gsn.org/

EdWeb is devoted to exploring and cataloging how the Internet can be used in the classroom. This site includes information on innovative uses of the Internet in education, electronic mailing lists of teachers in a wide variety of fields, and a list of links to K-12 schools which have their own Web sites.

International WWW Schools Registry

http://web66.coled.umn.edu/schools.html

A directory of thousands of elementary and secondary schools in more than 50 countries that have Web sites.

Web 66: A K-12 World Wide Web Project

http://web66.coled.umn.edu/

Route 66 is an old highway that traverses America and has been made famous by the authors, painters, poets, and songwriters who have told of their adventures while traveling along the road. Web 66 is a project to promote the use of the Internet in elementary and secondary education. The site highlights innovative classroom projects on the Internet and also includes a directory of hundreds of schools around the world that have their own Web sites.

PenPals

With the advent of electronic mail and the Internet many American schools have established electronic PenPal relationships with schools around the world. Activities range from exchanging messages to developing joint classroom projects. Below is a list of organizations and Internet resources which can help establish PenPal relationships with schools in the United States.

Center for Civil Society International	http://www.friends-partners.org/~ccsi/penhome.htm
Class-toClass Exchanges	http://www.peacecorps.gov/www/dp/resource/oed2.html
Keypals International	http://www.collegebound.com/keypals/

Pen Pal Planet	E-mail: ppplanet@epix.net
Sister Schools International	E-mail: WINFREF@mail.firn.edu
Intercultural E-mail Classroom Connections	http://www.stolaf.edu/network/iecc/
Internet School Linkage Program	http://www.friends-partners.org/~harmony/

The last reference above is to a new program of Project Harmony (based in Waitsfield, Vermont) that will establish relationships between schools in the NIS and the U.S. to develop jointly curriculum and other projects. As part of the Internet School Linkage Program the schools will create their own Web sites and publish the curriculum they develop.

Ukrainian Sites

Project for Economic Reform in Ukraine

gopher://ftp.std.com:70/11/nonprofits/Sabre.Foundation.Inc/Ukraine.FAQ.Plus/Organizations/United.States/Project.for.Economic.Reform.in.Ukraine-PERU/Kiev.Library.Holdings

PERU is a project of the Kennedy School of Government at Harvard University, begun in 1990 in response to a request by Ukrainian policy makers to help with reform of the economy of Ukraine. The site includes a list of all the books in PERU's library in Kyiv.

Supreme Rada

http://www.Rada.Kiev.UA/welcome.html

The Web site of Ukraine's Supreme Rada includes the text of some laws which have been passed by the legislature and summaries of others.

Ukraine: FAQ Plus

http://www.std.com/sabre/UKRAINE.html

(in English)

A variety of Web sites related to Ukraine are indexed in this directory. Subjects include:

- Economics, including a ling to a site that describes work of the International Ukrainian Economic Association, a scholarly association co-sponsored by Temple University in the U.S. and the National Academy of Sciences in Ukraine.
- Business and commerce, with descriptions of USAID projects in Ukraine.
- Organizations, which contains links to a variety of international institutions active in or connected with Ukraine, including, the Canadian Institute of Ukrainian Studies, the Ukrainian Legal Foundation, and the American-Ukrainian Advisory Committee.

Ukrainet

http://www.ukrainet.org/
(in English)
This Web site is a directory of Ukrainian-related Web sites and internet resources. Much of it is still under construction (including the business and economics sections), but it currently contains many links to news services, publications, and organizations, both Ukrainian and foreign.

Ukrainian Canadian Professional and Business Association

http://www.worldlink.ca/ucpbf/
(in English)
This site provides information on a variety of activities related to Canadian/Ukrainian partnerships. UCPBA-sponsored conferences and conventions in Canada are publicized here, as well as Canadian/Ukrainian joint ventures (a short index), a description of what the association does, and a brief listing of Ukrainian-related Internet sites. Unfortunately, most of the links in the "Ukrainian-related News & Information Sources" section are outdated and therefore, unusable.

Ukrainian Research Institute

http://www.sabre.org/huri/
(in English)
The Ukrainian Research Institute, located at Harvard University, provides resources for students studying Ukrainian language, literature, and history. This site is mainly a description of the programs of study available and organizations affiliated with the institute; however, the publications section allows the user to access online versions (until 1996) of "Perspectives on Contemporary Ukraine," a journal that features scholarly articles on

subjects ranging from Jewish life in Ukraine to an interview with Dr. Oleh Havrylyshyn, a Ukrainian economist working with the IMF. Also available at this site is a description of the Harvard Ukraine Business Initiative project, which is dedicated to fostering the development of a market economy in Ukraine. Contained in the HUBI section are instructions on how to subscribe to their publication, "The Ukrainian Legal and Economic Bulletin," as well as contact names and addresses for HUBI staff at Harvard.

Ukrainian WWW Links

http://www.infoukes.com/wwwlinks/

A directory of hundreds of WWW sites that are either in Ukraine or contain information related to Ukraine.

UN Development Project, Kyiv

http://www.un.kiev.ua/current_index.html

This site is dedicated to the United Nations Development Project in Ukraine. It includes lists of the UN's completed and current projects. The "Country Strategy Notes" section covers the issues associated with development particular to Ukraine, and uses economic performance indicators to determine the strategy for the nation's development.

University of Kyiv

http://www.univ.kiev.ua/

This home page for Ukraine's largest academic institution is surprisingly in English. The site is devoted to descriptions of the university and its departments—including the economics department—but there is not much here beyond contact information (number of students and professors, telephone numbers for administrative offices and professors), and accessing the server can be very slow. However, the site was only created in March 1997 and much of it still remains under construction. In time, it will surely grow and contain more information on the activities and projects of the economics department.

Miscellaneous

Center for International Private Enterprise

http://www.cipe.org/

CIPE is an affiliate of the U.S. Chamber of Commerce (see below) which has projects to promote private enterprise and market-oriented economic reform in 50 countries around the globe. Available at this site are articles from CIPE's quarterly journal *Economic Reform Today* such as "Securing Property Rights: The Foundation of Markets" and "Market Institutions and Democracy." A number of articles are available online in Russian.

Corruption Ranking

http://www.gwdg.de/~uwvw/icr.htm

A joint project of the Transparency Institute and Gottingen University in Germany, the Corruption Ranking is an annual "attempt to assess the level at which corruption is perceived by people working for multinational firms and institutions as impacting on commercial and social life." For the purpose of the surveys, corruption was defined as the misuse of public power for private benefit. The 1996 poll included 54 countries, with New Zealand listed as the least corrupt country and Nigeria and Pakistan as the most corrupt. There is also a table which includes the results of three polls dating back to the early 80's.

Ethical Business

http://www.arq.co.uk/ethicalbusiness/

Founded in 1995, the Ethical Business Web site is "for people interested in ethical and environmental business initiatives and the complex ethical and environmental issues that business faces." The site is maintained by Craig Mackenzie, a researcher with the Morality and Market Project at Bath University in England. The site consists mostly of links to other organizations which focus on ethical business, academic departments that study the issue, and "ethical" investment funds. There is also a small section which contains articles and papers on the general topic of ethical business, including a series of articles about a controversy surrounding the cosmetics firm, The Body Shop, which is one of the featured company profiles at the Biz/ed site (http://bizednet.bris.ac.uk:8080/home.htm).

International Organizations on the World Wide Web

http://www2.echo.lu/other/inter.html

This file is a list of links to home pages of international (mostly intergovernmental) organizations.

Internet FAQ

http://www.irex.ru

(Russian)

IREX, which has helped numerous NIS scholars and non-governmental organizations get connected to the Internet, has uploaded a Russian-language general introduction to the Internet. The *Internet FAQ* (Frequently Asked Questions) includes a brief overview of e-mail and the Internet, a listing of some of the major Internet providers in the NIS, and a list of organizations that offer technical assistance to NIS scholars and NGOs seeking Internet access.

Uniform Commercial Code

http://www.law.cornell.edu/ucc/ucc.table.html

At the heart of the market economy are contracts between buyers and sellers under which both parties have rights and obligations. One of the cornerstones of contract law in the U.S. is the Uniform Commercial Code (U.C.C.), which has been adopted, at least in part, by every state in the U.S. The Code, which is very well presented at this site, is split into nine sections, including:

- Sales
- Leases
- Negotiable Instruments
- Bank Deposits and Collections
- Funds Transfers
- Letters of Credit
- Bulk Transfers and Bulk Sales
- Warehouse Receipts, Bills of Lading, and Other Documents of Title
- Investment Securities
- Secured Transactions; Sales of Accounts and Chattel Paper

Each of these sections is further subdivided. For instance the section on Sales, includes subsections on:

- Short Title, General Construction, and Subject Matter
- Form, Formation, and Readjustment of Contract
- General Obligation and Construction of Contract

- Title, Creditors, and Good Faith Purchasers
- Performance
- Breach, Repudiation, and Excuse
- Remedies

In reading through these sections, one gains an understanding of the legal framework which underpins a market economy and the rights and responsibilities of the parties involved in a commercial transaction. Throughout the U.C.C. the viewer can view definitions of terms such as "Good faith," "Acceptance," "Contract for sale," "Termination," etc.

World Resources 1996-97

http://www.wri.org/wri/wr-96-97/

World Resources 1996-97: A Guide to the Global Environment is an annual publication produced by the World Resources Institute, the UN Environment Programme, the U.N. Development Programme, and the World Bank. The 1996-97 edition focused on the urban environment and included more than 160 tables of data.

World Survey of Economic Freedom

http://www.freedomhouse.org/Econ/TOC.HTM

The annual Survey of Economic Freedom ranks the economic policy of countries based on six factors:

- freedom to hold and transfer property
- freedom to earn a living
- freedom to operate a business
- freedom to invest one's earnings
- freedom to trade internationally
- freedom to participate in the market economy

For each of these categories countries are given a score of 1-3. The scores are tabulated and a country's economy is categorized as free, partly free, mostly not free, and not free.

The survey is conducted by Freedom House, a non-partisan organization which seeks to promote democracy around the world. Freedom House was founded in 1941 by Eleanor Roosevelt and Wendell Wilkie, who had just lost a presidential election to Eleanor's husband, to promote a U.S. foreign policy that more actively opposed Nazi Germany. Available at this site is Freedom House's annual *Survey of Political Freedom and Survey of Press Freedom.*

Electronic Mailing Lists

Electronic mailing lists are one of the most fun, interesting, and easy-to-use resources on the Internet. They are so popular because they rely on the simplest Internet technology: e-mail. Virtually anyone with e-mail—from Atlanta to Almaty, from Zanesville to Zagorsk—can participate in an electronic mailing list.

Functionally, electronic mailing lists can operate as a do-it-yourself news service, a continual seminar, a hobby group, or special interest society. They can consist of as few as 15 or 20 people to upwards of 1,000.

Technically speaking, an electronic mailing list is a software program installed on a host computer connected to the Internet with the following two features:

- an automatic mechanism whereby individuals may add or remove their name from the electronic mailing list;
- an automatic mechanism whereby a message posted to the list of subscribers is sent simultaneously to each subscriber.

Several software programs exist that automate this process. Three of the most common are Listserv, Listproc, and Majordomo. The first has become so common that it has almost become a synonym for any electronic mailing list. In other words, a person might say, "I just signed up to a listserv for fans of Nirvana."

Just as a good printed magazine creates a kind of community among its loyal readers and letters-to-the-editor writers, so do listservs create "virtual communities." The disadvantage of the electronic version is that it lacks graphics—messages are text only. But its advantages are the low cost, ease and speed of communication: it is as simple for a "listserv" to link 10 people all living in the Boston area, as 10 people living in Boston, Novosibirsk, Nairobi and Buenos Aires. There are no "long distance" charges for an e-mail message. As a result, today there are thousands of listservs and news groups, linking millions of individuals sharing specific interests around the world.

Like magazines, listservs serve as a forum where subscribers share ideas in common or post announcements. Unlike magazines, a group discussion can start within seconds of the posting of a message. Also, unlike a magazine, "clipping" and saving an item—or forwarding it to somebody else—is a matter of just a few keystrokes, and just as many seconds. No scissors, no filing, no addressing of envelopes, no stamps, no trip to the mailbox. When it is this easy to bounce information between people, you can imagine how many things get passed on that never made it out of the out-box in the past.

Posting questions is one of the most useful aspects of listservs. It is fascinating to see a listserv member post a question that seems rather arcane or unlikely to be answered—only to see four or five excellent answers to the question come back within hours. (It is customary to send answers to the whole list if you think the question is of general interest, but only to the person who asked, if the question was a narrow one.)

Finally, since many people who are members of e-mail lists are active users of the Internet and frequently pass on tips and discoveries, subscribing to a listserv is an excellent way to learn about other Internet resources in your area of interest.

Looking for Lists

There are a great many electronic mailing lists and those mentioned in this section are undoubtedly only some of the best that exist. There are places on the Internet, however, to search for lists of all kinds. Three good ones are given in this section.

Resources for Economists on the Internet (EconFAQ)

http://wueconb.wustl.edu/EconFAQ/EconFAQ.html

The EconFAQ includes a section on electronic mailing lists that is broken down by subject. It includes directions on how to subscribe and, in some cases, provides very brief information about the type of discussion the list carries.

Liszt

http://www.liszt.com/

A list of lists, Listz is a searchable database of 23,000 electronic mailing lists. A search for "economic" produced 140 lists. A search returns the name of the list, information on how to subscribe, and sometimes a brief description of the list.

Mailbase

http://www.mailbase.ac.uk/

Mailbase is a listserv software that is used predominantly in the United Kingdom. The Mailbase website allows one to search all mailbase lists (many of which don't show up in other 'lists of lists'). The Mailbase site also includes browsable archives for many of the mailbase lists.

Economic Education Lists

Business-SL

This list is for students around the world studying business and economics. Students join the list by having their teacher first register their class. Then the students join the Intro-SL list where they learn basic listserv etiquette and procedures. They can then join the Business-SL list.

Teachers can register their classes by sending a message to trobb@cc.kyoto-su.ac.jp with the following information:

- Your name and institution
- Number of students
- Duration of class term
- Name of the node the students will use (the part following the '@' mark).

The teacher will be placed on a special list just for teachers involved with the project. They will also receive a document which describes the project in more detail and an orientation handout for students.

Central European Regional Research Organization

CERRO, based in Vienna, is a major repository of economic research about Eastern Europe. It used to be more active a couple of years ago.

List address:	cerro-l@aearn.aco.net
To subscribe, send this message:	subscribe cerro-l firstname lastname
to:	listserv@aearn.edvz.univie.ac.at

Community Economic Development in Developed Countries

A discussion list on the trends in community economic development. The focus is on what communities can do to gain access to markets and investment.

List address:	ced-net@sfu.ca
To subscribe, send this message:	subscribe ced-net
to:	majordomo@sfu.ca

Discussion on the transition in Eastern Europe & former Soviet Union

A primarily U.K.-based discussion group that is not as active as it could be with the participation of economists from Eastern Europe and the ex-USSR. Back messages posted to the list are archived at:
http://www.mailbase.ac.uk/lists-a-e/east-west-research/archive.html

List address:	east-west-research@mailbase.ac.uk
To subscribe, send this message:	subscribe east-west-research firstname lastname
to:	mailbase@mailbase.ac.uk

Econ-business-educators

Managed by Richard Young who maintains the Biz/Ed Web site, this list averages around 10-15 messages a month. Young does a good job of telling other list members about new resources he has found.

List address:	econ-business-educators@mailbase.ac.uk
To subscribe, send this message:	subscribe econ-business-educators firstname lastname
to:	mailbase@mailbase.ac.uk

Economic History of the Eastern Bloc

See what Western academics are saying about the old communist economic system. Archives are available at:
http://cs.muohio.edu/Archives/eh.eastbloc/

List address:	eh.eastbloc@cs.muohio.edu
To subscribe, send this message:	subscribe eh.eastbloc firstname lastname
to:	lists@cs.muohio.edu

Family and Consumer Economists, Consumer Educators

This list has had light traffic in recent months.

List address:	conssci@lsv.uky.edu
To subscribe, send this message:	subscribe conssci firstname lastname
to:	listserv@lsv.uky.edu

History of Economics Society List

For scholars interested in the history of economics. The list features discussion and monthly guest editorials, references to new Web sites, and sharing of ideas about teaching economics history.

List address:	hes@cs.muohio.edu
To subscribe, send this message:	subscribe hes firstname lastname
to:	lists@cs.muohio.edu

Innovation in Instruction of Economics

Not a very active list. The list includes teachers from Brazil, the Netherlands, Germany, and New Zealand.

List address:	i3econ@ccvm.sunysb.edu
To subscribe, send this message:	subscribe i3econ firstname lastname
to:	listserv@ccvm.sunysb.edu

NAEEnet

A private list for members of the National Association of Economic Educators, but non-members can contact the list manager, Abbejean Kehler (kehler.1@osu.edu), to ask whether they can be added.

Scout Report for Business & Economics

The Business & Economics Report is a bi-weekly electronic bulletin consisting of excellent and brief reviews of Web sites, electronic mailing lists and journals, and online databases related to business or economics. It is published by the Internet Scout Project, based at the University of Wisconsin-Madison's Department of Computer Sciences.

To subscribe, send this message:	subscribe SRBUSECON
to:	scoutlst@cs.wisc.edu

Teach-econ

Teach-Econ is a list for teachers of economics (primarily at the college level) to share their ideas and experiences. A browsable archive of back messages is available at: http://wuecon.wustl.edu/~tchecndg/

List address:	tch-econ@majordomo.elon.edu
To subscribe, send the message:	subscribe tch-econ
to:	majordomo@majordomo.elon.edu

US-NIS Lists

These lists are good places to meet individuals, scholars, and organizations active or interested in the NIS and Eastern Europe.

CenAsia

People with projects in Central Asia, as well as those with a general interest in the region, will find the CenAsia list to be an excellent resource. CenAsia includes: announcements of meetings and job openings; news of organizations working in the region; leads to other Internet resources related to the region; and references to print materials, such as journals and dictionaries. Because the community of Westerners interested or working in Central Asia is relatively small, many members know each other and the ethic of sharing information is strong. A frequent use of the list involves queries about e-mail addresses and sources of connectivity in the region.

CenAsia is also a political discussion list, and unlike some discussion lists on the Internet, is distinguished by the high quality of discussion and the background and expertise of its participants. Academics such as James Critchlow and Edward Keenan of Harvard and Barnett Rubin of Columbia and the Council on Foreign Relations are joined by articulate people from the region, many of whom are also scholars. Archives of CenAsia are available at: http://www.soros.org/tajkstan.html

List address:	cenasia@vm1.mcgill.ca
To subscribe, send this message:	subscribe cenasia firstname lastname
to:	listserv@vm1.mcgill.ca

CEEMAN

This is a private list for members of the Central and Eastern Europe Management network, which links rectors and professors of Management institutes in Eastern Europe and the former USSR. Although the list is private, you can send a message asking to be added to CEEMAN to the list manager Dennis McConnell at: mac@maine.maine.edu

CivilSoc

Sponsored by the Center for Civil Society International, CivilSoc is a source of news and resources related to the development of civil society institutions in the NIS. It includes announcements about projects by U.S. organizations in the NIS, profiles of NIS NGOs (non-governmental organizations), grant announcements, and print and electronic resources. Many subscribers are active in NGO projects in the NIS. CivilSoc averages 4-5 messages a week, with an average monthly volume of 50-70 kilobytes. Posts are kept concise so as to reduce cost for subscribers in the NIS. Many of the messages posted to CivilSoc are archived at CCSI's Web site: http://www.friends-partners.org/~ccsi/

List address:	civilsoc@solar.cini.utk.edu
To subscribe, send this message:	subscribe civilsoc firstname lastname
to:	listproc@solar.cini.utk.edu

EE-Econ

Discussion of general economics issues related to Central and Eastern Europe and the NIS.

List address:	ee-econ@cep.yale.edu
To subscribe, send this message:	sub ee-econ your-email-address
to:	majordomo@cep.yale.edu

EE-Higher-Ed

Discussion of issues related to higher education in Central and Eastern Europe and the NIS.

List address:	ee-higher-ed@cep.yale.edu
To subscribe, send this message:	sub ee-higher-ed your-email-address
to:	majordomo@cep.yale.edu

Friends

Companion of the innovative Friends and Partners Internet site established by Greg Cole in Knoxville, Tennessee, and Natasha Bulashova in Puschino, Russia, Friends is a great place to meet people and learn what is happening in a wide range of U.S.-NIS citizen activity. It includes many announcements which appear on other lists, but it also includes messages from individuals who introduce themselves or ask questions about where to find different types of information. The list is also used to announce additions to the Friends and Partners World Wide Web site. Unlike most other electronic mailing lists which consist of messages posted by different people to the list, Friends is a "digested" list. This means messages posted to the list are combined into one file which is distributed to subscribers every two or three days. These "Digests" include a table of contents at the top that lists the sender of each message and the subject line. The Friends' Digests are usually around 30 kilobytes in size.

List address:	friends@solar.cini.utk.edu
To subscribe, send this message:	susbcribe friends firstname lastname
to:	listproc@solar.cini.utk.edu

Grants

Maintained by Marek Tiits of the Institute of Baltic Studies in Tartu, Estonia, Grants is of interest primarily to people in Eastern Europe and the NIS. The list consists solely of announcements about grant programs for which CEE and NIS residents can apply. The list averages 5-7 messages a month.

List address:	grants@ibs.ee
To subscribe, send this message:	subscribe grants firstname lastname
to:	listserv@ibs.ee

Ukes-news

Primarily the North American-Ukrainian community's on-line bulletin board. Many Ukes-news subscribers travel to Ukraine regularly and have projects or business deals there. Ukes-news includes announcements of Ukraine-related events in the U.S. and Canada, some discussion of current events in Ukraine, and occasional reports by Ukrainian organizations, including the *Ukrainian Arts Monitor* and *The Rukh Insider*. The list includes people who are very knowledgeable about e-mail and the Internet and who are also very willing to help; it is a good place to post questions about e-mail access in Ukraine. Although there is some discussion on Ukes-news, it is primarily a list for posting announcements. Discussion of Ukrainian related topics is done mostly on the other Ukes list, Ukes-social which is described in the materials you receive when you subscribe to Ukes-news.

List address:	announce@infoukes.com
To subscribe, send a message with the word "subscribe" in the Subject line	
to:	announce-request@infoukes.com

Women-East-West

Women-East-West is sponsored by the Network of East-West Women, which works to promote the formation of independent women's movements in Eastern Europe and the former USSR. NEWW has a project to distribute modems and provide e-mail training for women's organizations in Eastern Europe and the NIS. As a result, the Women-East-West list includes an interesting variety of messages from women in the region introducing themselves and their organizations. In the last couple of months the list has also included monthly reports from NIS NGOs, including "Femina" in Naberezhnye Chelny, Zonta International Tartu Club in Estonia, and the

Association of Independent Women's Initiatives in Tver, Russia. The list averages 3-5 messages a week.

List address:	women-east-west@igc.apc.org
To subscribe, send this message:	subscribe women-east-west
to:	majordomo@igc.apc.org

Usenet and News Groups

Internet host computers nearly always include access to the Usenet network, which can be thought of as an electronic newswire service. Each Internet site (such as a university, a business, or an Internet service provider) on the Usenet network subscribes to a specific set of "news groups," selected according to the interests of those with accounts at that particular site. There is, for example, a Usenet news group named k12.ed.business. If a host computer on the Usenet network in Sydney, Australia, for example, chooses to subscribe to this news group, it means that all of its Australian account holders will be able to view and post messages to k12.ed.business. Likewise, messages posted by an Australian to the news group will reach all other Internet users whose host computer takes the k12.ed.business "news feed."

The Usenet links perhaps as many as 20,000 or more news groups, which are also known as conferences, bulletin boards, forums, or chat rooms. Usenet member sites may subscribe to all existing news groups, or to only a portion of them. The topics on which news groups focus range from banking to baroque music and everything in between.

There are four main differences between news groups and electronic mailing lists:

- Electronic mailing lists give those setting them up more control, both over membership subscription, which can be automatic or subject to the approval of the list administrator, and over content. List administrators can intercept and not send on messages they deem to be inappropriate.
- News groups potentially reach larger numbers of people. A message posted to a popular Usenet news group conceivably reaches every account holder of every Internet service provider that subscribes to that particular news group. This number can run in the tens of millions of people.
- There is a big difference, however, between messages that come automatically into your e-mail inbox through an electronic mailing list, and messages posted to a news group folder which you must open in order to read. For this reason, messages posted on electronic mailing lists are much more likely to be read.
- Discussion or "chat" groups which require being able to review and respond to a series of messages posted by different people over a period of time can be more suited to a news group than an electronic mailing list. People tend to delete old e-mail; or they lose track of it among scores of

other messages on different topics. In contrast, news group posts are automatically collected and saved in that news group's folder for periods of days, weeks, or even months—to be read and answered at the reader's convenenience. An additional bonus of Usenet is that messages can be "threaded," so that all the responses to a message with the subject line "It's raining in Seattle, again!" can be grouped together. Threading also helps in managing discussions involving a lot of people and messages.

How is Usenet organized?

Usenet news group names or addresses are organized in a hierarchical structure, usually containing two or three terms. The first term in the name is known as the "top-level hierarchy." Some of the most common top-level Usenet hierarchies and the discussion topics they refer to are listed below:

alt	an anarchic collection of subjects
biz	business products and services
comp	computer hardware, software, etc.
humanities	literature, fine arts, and other humanities
k12	K-12 education
misc	miscellaneous topics
rec	recreational topics, such as sports, games, hobbies, etc.
relcom	Russian news groups
sci	pure and applied sciences
soc	social issues
talk	discussion and debate
ukr	Ukrainian news groups

Under each of these top-level hierarchies there are further categories and further sub-categories. For example:

- sci.econ is a news group which focuses on economics;
- alt.current-events is a news group category under which there are the alt.current-events.russia and alt.current-events.usa sub-categories.

Much more could be said about news groups and the Usenet. Readers wishing to learn more about this interesting and useful aspect of the Internet are encouraged to visit the following Web site for more information:

http://www.netannounce.org/news.announce.newusers/

News Groups for Economic Educators

If you are connected to the World Wide Web, but don't now which news groups your Internet service provider carries, you can find out by pointing your Web browser to the location on your host computer which maintains such a list. (This is usually easily obtained from your Internet service provider.) If you don not find a news group that interests you, there are a couple of places you can go to try to find ones that do. You can then request that your Internet service provider subscribe to these news groups, too.

Lists of widely-distributed news groups, along with a one-line description of each one, are regularly posted to the news.lists news group. There are also several Web sites which include lists and search mechanisms for news groups, including www.dejanews.com and www.hotbot.com.

Bill Goffe who maintains the Resources for Economists on the Internet Web site (listed in the "Internet Sites, Clearinghouse" section) keeps track of all the economics-related news groups. As of the summer of 1997 the URL for Goffe's news group reviews was:

http://wueconb.wustl.edu/EconFAQ/node471.html

There appear to be three news groups that would be of primary interest to economics educators:

- sci.econ, discussion in economics, averages 100 messages a day;
- sci.econ.research, averages 5-10 messages a day, and the posts are much more focused and professional than sci.econ;
- k12.ed.business, a low volume list that is just waiting for economic educators to start networking.

Another useful resource is ClariNet. ClariNet is an electronic newspaper that is delivered via Usenet under the hierarchy clari. It consists of wire service stories from news agencies such as Agence France Presse, United Press International, and Reuters. Some of the more interesting news groups are: clari.biz.briefs, clari.biz.economy, clari.biz.features, and clari.biz.industry. Under the last category there are 51 separate news groups for specific industries. ClariNet is a fee-based service, so many ISP's may carry only a small number of its news groups. For more information about ClariNet and how to get your ISP to subscribe to the news groups you want, visit the ClariNet Web site at: http://www.clari.net.

Searching for Information on the World Wide Web: Search Engines

The lack of centralization in the Internet means that there is no single online catalog and there are no indexes to *all* the materials on the Internet. In fact, gaining access to the Internet has been compared to entering a vast library in which all the books have been dumped off the shelves, mixed together, and strewed on the floor. But it is not really as disorganized as this suggests. In recent years people have developed software that structures collections of materials and helps users find documents located on different computers on the Internet. Some of these so-called "search engines" are described below.

But even after you learn about search engines and how to use them, it remains true that a bit of random wandering often doesn't hurt. In fact, as mentioned in the introduction, the best way to learn about the Internet is to get online and do just that: wander. Web sites often have links to pages on similar topics, so finding one page on a certain topic often means that you can jump with a click of your mouse to different sites on the same topic. Rather than thinking of the Internet as a vast room with books all over the floor, think of it as very large library with instantaneous access to thousands of collections. One room can lead to many different rooms. On the Internet you can follow links on similar topics, or after following a few links you could end up on a page completely different from the first page you started —just with a few clicks of the mouse. The possibilities are huge and only discovered by, in effect, walking some of the corridors of the Internet. Exploring the Internet is a process that always combines elements of deliberate searching and accidental discovery.

So what is a "search engine"?

An Internet search engine is a piece of software residing on a server linked to the Internet that continually "trolls" the Internet and adds links to new files it finds to its database. Most search engines have three basic parts:

- An automated search device (sometimes called a "spider") that automatically searches the Internet periodically.
- A searchable database where this information resides (containing links, titles, text, etc.).

- A public Web site which allows "outsiders" to search and access this information.

Depending on the software used, search engines vary in the size of their databases, how up-to-date they are, and how easy they make it for users to find files on specific topics, using key words or phrases. As the Internet now links millions of files on thousands of servers around the world, a good search engine needs to be very powerful in order to search each of these servers systematically for files containing specific terms or kinds of information.

Search engines are improving all the time, making it possible for the user to specify limits on the number of files that are "returned" and to focus the search in a way that ensures that those files that are returned are in fact closely related to the search topic. Searches that are too general or too broad simply turn up too many documents to be useful. Additionally, some search engines now offer the ability to do searches in a number of languages other than English, including Russian.

Following are two of the search engines available on the Web for Russian language users:

AltaVista (Russian)

http://www.comptek.ru/alta.html

This is a recent development at AltaVista, one of the most popular search engines on the Web, developed by the engineers at Digital Equipment. This engine appears to run separately from the main AltaVista site (noted below) and oddly enough isn't mentioned at that site. It only accepts search terms in Cyrillic so users must have software on their computers able to generate Cyrillic characters. Unlike the AltaVista main site, it can limit searches to servers based in Russia (those with the .su and .ru suffix).

APORT Search Engine

http://russia.agama.com/aport/

This Russian-language Internet search engine also performs searches in English, or both Russian and English at the same time, and will list search findings ("hits") in Russian or English. The site's home page is in Russian and contains a good "help section" with detailed instructions on how to construct search strategies. Users can view the site via all major Cyrillic font encodings: Windows, KOI-8, Mac, and DOS.

Popular search engines

Some of the most popular search engines today are listed below:

AltaVista	http://www.altavista.digital.com
Excite	http://www.excite.com
HotBot	http://www.hotbot.com
Infoseek Ultra	http://ultra.infoseek.com
Lycos	http://www.lycos.com
MetaCrawler	http://metacrawler.cs.washington.edu
MotherLoad	http://www.cosmix.com/motherload/insane
NlightN	http://www.nlightn.com
Savvy Search	http://guaraldi.cs.colostate.edu:2000
WebCrawler	http://webcrawler.com
Yahoo!	http://www.yahoo.com

Some of the engines above have specific strengths. NlightN, for example, offers Web searching plus searches for titles of printed books, magazine and journal articles, news archives, and reference works. MotherLoad allows searches of a number of other search engines simultaneously. It also allows searches of the entire line of Ziff-Davis computer publications, the Library of Congress, and the DejaNews database of Usenet group postings. For a good, current listing of search engines and directories available on the Internet, InterNIC provides such a list at:

http://www.internic.net/tools/search.html

The important thing is to find a search engine, out of the many available on the Web, which works for you, and to spend a few minutes familiarizing yourself with its search functions. Search engines can vary, too, in whether they use "Boolean operators" (AND, OR, and NOT) and have other features. (George Boole was a British mathematician and logician of the mid-nineteenth century.) This said, if you learn how to use one search engine, the skills you learn there will most likely transfer easily to another one.

AltaVista

The following examples are based on the **AltaVista** search engine, one of the most popular in use today. It was developed by Digital Equipment as a way to demonstrate the speed of its computers. For additional information on AltaVista, including more examples of different search techniques, go to its home page, using the address above, and click on "Help."

In order to perform what AltaVista refers to as a "Simple Query," you simply enter a word or words in the Online Search Box at AltaVista's home page. For example:

unemployment France	Submit

Often, a simple subject search on the Web retrieves an overwhelming number of documents. For example, a search on unemployment France in AltaVista recently retrieved "about 127,190" items. The search engine also reported that it had found 161,305 documents containing the word unemployment only and 1,175,718 containing the word France only! Clearly searches like this are almost worthless.

Fortunately, AltaVista provides several mechanisms for narrowing or focusing a search:

Quotation marks

"unemployment in France"

Searching with quotation marks directs the search engine to find every document containing the exact phrase placed within quotes: e.g., "unemployment in France" (i.e., the three words must be immediately adjacent to each other and occur in the order given).

When this search was attempted in AltaVista, the computer returned only 24 documents—a much more manageable number! This is one example of how a simple technique dramatically focuses the search on a specific type of document you want.

Plus and Minus Signs

"unemployment in France" +1997
"unemployment in France" -1997

AltaVista allows you to require that specified words or phrases be included in every item your search retrieves. The plus sign (+) tells the database that 1997 is a required word in any document retrieved, thus allowing you to narrow your search to relatively recent documents. Similarly, the minus sign (-) tells the search engine to omit any files cointaining a certain term—i.e., to list all files containing the term "unemployment in France," *except* those which contain the term 1997. Note that there is *no space* between the plus or minus signs and 1997.

Segment Searching

You can restrict your search to a specific part or *segment* of a document, such as its URL, title, hyperlinks, image, etc. This is especially helpful if you know one or more terms in the title of a document. For example, a document with a title such as, "Unemployment in France: Structural Causes," would be found with either of these simple commands:

title:"Unemployment in France"

title:"Structural Causes"

Again, note that there is *no space* after the term title:

Truncation

"unemployment in France" +south*

The use of the asterisk (*) tells the database to look for any document containing the term unemployment in France as well as any word that *begins* with south, with a maximum of 5 letters following the word "stem". This search would find anything with the phrase unemployment in France and the words: south, southeast, southwest, southern, southerner, southerly, etc...

A word of caution—if you're not careful, truncation can retrieve many irrelevant documents. For example, you want to find sing, singers or singing, so you enter sing* as your search term. This search will find all of the above, but also words such as singular, single, singe, etc. The asterisk may also be used within a word, which can be useful if a term has various spellings. For example, arch*eology will find both archaeology and archeology.

Capitalization

AltaVista recommends that capitalization be avoided in most instances. Lower case searches are "case-insensitive," meaning that a search on antarctic would find both Antarctic and antarctic. This is not true, however, for searches based on words with upper case letters in them. Use of any upper case letters forces an "exact case match." Thus, a search on Antarctic would exclude any variants on the entire word, such as ANTARCTIC.

Ranking

For Simple Queries, AltaVista will rank the results based on a scoring algorithm; documents with a higher score appear at the head of the ranking list. A document has a higher score if the following hold:

- Your search words or phrases are found in the first few words of the document (for example, in the title of a Web page or in the headers of Usenet news articles).
- Your search words or phrases are found close to one another in the document.
- The document contains more than one instance of the query word or phrase.

Advanced Searches in AltaVista

If you click on the box that says "Advanced Search," you will be taken to a screen that asks a question like this: "Selection Criteria: Please use Advanced Syntax (AND, OR, NOT, NEAR)."

Using "and," "or," "not," "near"

AND e.g., "unemployment in France" AND elections

The word "AND" ensures that *both* unemployment in France *and* elections are present in the items retrieved.

OR e.g., "unemployment in France" OR elections

"OR" tells the database that at least one of the terms must be present in the items retrieved.

AND NOT e.g., "unemployment in France" AND NOT elections

"AND NOT" excludes search terms; in effect, it works like the minus sign in Alta Vista's Simple Queries search mode. In this case, such a search would be one way to eliminate documents discussing the political ramifications of unemployment in France.

NEAR e.g., "unemployment in France" NEAR elections

"NEAR" specifies that your search terms must be within a certain number of words of each other. Most search engines use a default value for NEAR, such as within 25 words, but they also allow you to override the default and enter your own value. NEAR searches are often surprisingly successful.

Results Ranking Criteria

Some search engines allow you to prioritize search terms, by offering you something like a "Results Ranking Criteria Box." Words or phrases that you insert in the Results Ranking Criteria box will determine the ranking of the search results. High scores are assigned if the selected ranking word appears in the first few words of the document (i.e., in the title of a Web page or in a header), or if the document contains more than one instance or occurrence of the ranking word. If ranking is used, the results of a search are displayed in ranked order, with those items having a high score being listed first.

The best way to learn more about the techniques of search is to visit a powerful search engine, read the instructions they offer, and then try out a variety of search instructions. Remember, all search engines will have slightly different databases of information, and slightly different algorithms for ranking the results. This means if you can't find information on one search engine, try the same search on a different one. You'll be amazed at how specific your searches can be with just a few commands.

Appendixes

Appendix A.

Glossary

ASCII	American Standard Computer Information
Browser	Software installed on your computer to facilitate navigating on the World Wide Web. Two of the major browsers in use today are Netscape and Microsoft Explorer.
CEE	Central and Eastern Europe
Download	To copy a file from a "host" computer (or "server") on a network to a "local" or "client" computer that is connected to the network.
FAQ	Frequently Asked Questions, the name given to any document found at an Internet site listing a series of questions related to some issue and providing the answers.
FSU	Former Soviet Union
FTP	File Transfer Protocol. FTP sites are collections of files which are retrievable using a set of commands, such as "get," in the File Transfer Protocol. The first generation of Internet sites.
Home page	Usually the first document you see when you visit an organization's World Wide Web site.
Host	The computer on a network which runs programs for other computers ("clients") connected to it. Also called "server."
HTML	Hyper Text Markup Language. HTML is the formatting code for World Wide Web documents.
Hypertext	Text in a document on the World Wide Web which serves as a link to another document. A word that serves as hypertext will always be in a different color or in some other way look different from the rest of the text around it. Activating the hypertext link, by pressing Enter or clicking on it with a mouse, will take you to another document or menu of files.
ISP	Internet Service Provider. A commercial firm, a university, or any other organization offering connection to the Internet through its computers to customers who pay (sometimes) a monthly fee.

Listserv	An electronic mailing list, or the program that resides on a host computer and operates the automatic distribution of e-mail to a list of subscribers.
Lynx	A World Wide Web browser. Text only.
NIS	Newly Independent States of the former USSR.
Pointer	An Internet term which refers to a link, in either Gopher or World Wide Web, from one Internet site to another. Sometimes an Internet site is described as having "collected a good list of pointers," which means that site you can automatically visit a lot of other Internet sites.
Server	Same as host computer. (See "host" above.) On a network, a single program on the "server" computer, such as an e-mail program, is able to "serve" the many computers connected to it simultaneously. The computers that are "served" are sometimes referred to as "clients."
Snail Mail	The derisive term used for mail that is sent on paper in an envelope through the national postal service.
Telnet	An Internet utility which enables you to log-on to a remote computer.
Unix	The operating system of most networks and large computers.
Upload	To copy or send a file from a local computer to a network host computer or server.
URL	Uniform Resource Locator. The formal name for the address of a file or document on the Internet.
UUCP	UNIX to UNIX copy. An increasingly outdated e-mail system in which you read and compose messages off-line and you only go on-line when you upload and download e-mail messages.
WAIS	An Internet search utility.
World Wide Web	The latest generation of Internet site. Allows you to view and retrieve text, graphics, and audio files.
WWW	World Wide Web

Appendix B.

Understanding Electronic Mailing List Rules

Electronic mailing lists are so efficient because they are automated. This means subscribers sign up and sign off from a list by themselves. But because the procedures are so automated, first-time users sometimes have difficulty getting signed on (and off).

The procedure is very simple, if you remember one thing: all electronic mailing lists have two addresses: the List Subscription Address and the Message Posting Address.

The List Subscription Address

The List Subscription Address is the address to which you send a strictly prescribed message, requesting to sign on to (or to sign off of) a particular electronic mailing list. For Center for Civil Society International's CivilSoc list, this address is:

listproc@solar.cini.utk.edu

Usually the first part of a List Subscription Address indicates which software program is being used by a particular electronic mailing list. For example, here are three List Subscription Addresses, representing three different electronic list administration software programs:

listserv@pucc.princeton.edu
listproc@solar.cini.utk.edu
majordomo@rain.org

Sometimes one address can serve as the List Subscription Address for many different lists. (But *never* the Message Posting Address, which must be unique for each list.) For instance, the second address above, listproc@solar.cini.utk.edu, serves as the List Subscription Address for both CivilSoc and another electronic mailing list known as Friends.

The Message Posting Address

The Message Posting Address is the address to which you submit messages for re-transmission to everyone else, *once you have subscribed to the list.* If you participate in your list only to read the messages of others and you never submit a message of your own, you will never use this address. However, if you do occasionally wish to submit messages for the entire list, you will use this address each time you submit a message for general posting.

Here is an example of a message posting address:

civilsoc@solar.cini.utk.edu.

It is the address of Center for Civil Society International's electronic mailing list.

The first part of the address, the section before the @ symbol, is usually the name by which the list is known, and generally offers a pretty good clue about the list's focus. In the above example, Civilsoc is a list that focuses on news related to the growth of civil society in Russia and the NIS.

Subscribing to a List

Despite the different softwares, the process and syntax of subscribing to most electronic mailing lists are very similar. Typically, you are asked to send a simple e-mail message to the List Subscription Address which says, *all on one line*, that you want to subscribe to a specific electronic mailing list:

subscribe list-name your-first-name your-last-name

For example, if Ivan Turgenev wanted to subscribe to the CivilSoc mailing list, he would send an e-mail message containing this sentence:

subscribe civilsoc Ivan Turgenev

to this address:

listproc@solar.cini.utk.edu

Most e-mail software has a "Subject" line. Leave this line blank. Put your message in the "Message" area. It also usually does not matter whether you type letters in upper case or lower case.[1]

Once you have sent this message, you will receive a "welcome to the list" message acknowledging your subscription and a giving you directions for a variety of utilities, including how to post messages to the list and how to unsubscribe. **Save this message**. Once you are subscribed, you will begin to receive messages which always contain the Message Posting Address. But you won't see instructions again about how to unsubscribe. *So save them*.

Here's a typical electronic mailing list header:

Date: Wed, 4 July 1776
From: Benjamin Franklin <ben@poor.richard.almanac.com>
To: CivilSoc <civilsoc@solar.cini.utk.edu>
Subject: Good news from Philadelphia—Declaration of Independence from the British!

This header tells you that the message was posted to the CivilSoc list, of which you are now a member, and that it was sent by Benjamin Franklin.

Now suppose that you wanted to comment on this so-called "Declaration of Independence" that Franklin announced to everybody on the list. If you wanted to send a reply **only** to him, you would send your comment to:

ben@poor.richard.almanac.com

But if you wanted to open a discussion of Ben's Declaration, or invite comments on your opinion of Ben's Declaration from others on the list, then you would post your message to:

civilsoc@solar.cini.utk.edu

This is basically how an electronic mailing list works. It's a powerful communications vehicle—as you will see if you sign up to some of the lists described below and try them out for a time.

---

[1]Majordomo software does not require that you give your name; thus, Turgenev's message to a Majordomo list processor would simply read: **subscribe civilsoc**

Appendix C.

Understanding Internet Addresses and URLs

Internet addresses are constructed in a simple and logical fashion which, if understood, can help greatly to locate files whose addresses may have changed. This is especially so as Web sites get larger and larger, with thousands of files being organized at one site under scores of directories. If you understand the elements of a document's e-mail address, this will help you find it, especially if a site has recently be re-designed and the location of that document on the site has changed.

Every document on the Internet has a unique address, called a Uniform Resource Locator or URL. For example, the URL of the National Council on Economic Education is:

http://www.nationalcouncil.org/

That of Center for Civil Society International (CCSI) is:

http://www.friends-partners.org/~ccsi/ccsihome.html

There are three parts to a URL:

http:	//	www.friends-partners.org	/	~ccsi/ccsihome.html
format		*host computer*		*directory and file name*

The first part of the URL identifies the format of the file. There are about 10 different Internet formats. The most common include: http, gopher, ftp, telnet. URLs that begin with http: are World Wide Web documents. Those that begin with gopher: are obviously Gopher documents, and the same with FTP. In all probability, the great majority of documents you will see will be Web files beginning with http://

The second part of a URL (between the double forward slashes, "//", and the next single forward slash) contains the name, or address, of the computer (often called "host" or "server") on which the file is physically located. This usually corresponds to the "home page" address of a site. For example, the first URL above, http://www.nationalcouncil.org/, takes you to the home page of the National Council on Economic Education.

The home page of CCSI has a longer URL, because its home page is one of several on a computer which hosts home pages for a number of organizations like Center for Civil Society International. It is worth noting, too, that the computer at which CCSI has its site is in Tennessee. But this computer could be literally anywhere in the world. This is one of the wonders of the Internet: the host computer for an organization's Web site could be in Kuala Lumpur, Malaysia, even though the organization is in Seattle, WA.

For people interested to know in which country a host computer or server is located, the last part of the host computer address usually tells the story. Computers located in the U.S. typically have *no* country designation, but use a variety of endings, such as .edu, .com, or .gov. Web sites on computers based in *other* countries usually have a country abbreviation in their host computer addresses. For example,

.by	Belarus
.ee	Estonia
.lt	Lithuania
.lv	Latvia
.ru	Russia
.su	Soviet Union
.ua	Ukraine

The third part of a URL, after the first single forward slash "/", gives the directory and sub-directories under which a file is located at a particular computer. The forward slash sign ("/") separates directories. The term after the *last* forward slash in a URL is the name of the particular file. It is similar to the way files are named on PCs. For example if you use Word for Windows, a filename might look like this: c:\winword\letterhome.doc.

There are two things to remember about URLs:

- There are *no blank spaces* in a URL.
- *Capitalization matters* when typing a URL. Unlike e-mail addresses, which can be typed in either upper or lower case letters, a URL must be typed absolutely correctly or the World Wide Web browser can't find the document.

Appendix D. Finding Exchange Rates and Share Prices

Following are some World Wide Web sites which offer information on the prices of company shares and foreign exchange rates on international markets.

Currency

CEE & NIS Exchange Rates

http://www.omri.cz/Econ/ExchangeRates.html
OMRI maintains a regularly updated table of exchange rates of CEE and NIS currencies to the U.S. dollar.

Currency Converter

http://bin.gnn.com/cgi-bin/gnn/currency
This site is very simple to use. Just click on a currency and the Currency Converter will give you a list of all other currencies calculated relative to the one you selected.

Currencies of the World

http://pacific.commerce.ubc.ca/trade/currencies.html
This is a table of all the world's currencies. The table includes: the name of the currency; its basic denomination, i.e. dollar, franc, ruble; and the basic way in which a currency's value is determined, i.e. floating, valued against a basket of other currencies, tied to the dollar, etc.

Share Prices

These are sites which maintain regularly updated lists of links to WWW sites that have information related to stocks and stock markets.

EDGAR

http://www.sec.gov/edgarhp.htm
Maintained by the Securities and Exchange Commission, the U.S. government agency which regulates the stock market, EDGAR is an on-line

database of reports that companies are required to submit to the government. Included are annual reports of most American corporations (and some foreign) which describe a company's annual revenue and costs.

InvestorsEdge

http://www.investorsedge.com/

InvestorsEdge groups companies by industry.

Polish Stock Market

http://yogi.ippt.gov.pl/gielda/gielda.html

This site offers data on shares, bonds, financial results, and data from previous sessions. Information on shares is found in the "PGPW - rynek ascji" directory, for bonds, in the "WGPW - ryneck obligacji" directory, and for financial results, in the "WGPW - walory" directory.

Stock Markets around the world

http://www.yahoo.com/Business_and_Economy/Markets_and_Investments/Stocks/Stock_Exchanges

StockPlayer Resource Page

http://207.102.139.3/

A long list of links to WWW sites which are in some way related to the stock market. The list includes quite a few newsletters which specialize financial reporting.

StockMaster

http://www.stockmaster.com/

StockMaster includes data for many American companies. The list of stocks also serves as a links page for WWW sites of many American firms.

Yahoo!

http://www.yahoo.com/Economy/Markets_and_Investments/Stocks

List of stock markets around the world.

Appendix E. About Adobe Acrobat™

Adobe Acrobat™ is a program which allows a Website to display information in one format which it controls. The advantage of Adobe Acrobat is that one file can be displayed in different platforms: Windows, Macintosh, OS/2, and UNIX. In other words, if an Excel file with charts and graphs were in Adobe format, it would not need not be converted for each platform, as long as Adobe Acrobat™ had been installed first.

In order to view Adobe Acrobat™ files, they must be downloaded to the computer and opened with an Adobe Acrobat™ Reader. The Acrobat Reader is free to download and easy to install and use.

Downloading the Adobe Acrobat Reader

The Acrobat Reader can be obtained from the Adobe Website at http://www.adobe.com. From the Adobe home page, click on the "Get Acrobat Reader." This will bring you to the Acrobat page which will give you many choices. This page may list several versions of the reader, and the programs which can be used to create files in the reader format (.pdf). Pick one version of the reader.

After deciding on this, there is still a choice of language versions. Choose the version you wish, and download it from the Adobe Web site. The file size will be around 1.5 MB, which means that it could take as much as 10-15 minutes to download (using a 28.8 Kbps modem).

Listed below the language versions is an FTP address which can also be used to dowload the Adobe Acrobat™ reader. That address is: ftp://ftp.adobe.com/pub/adobe/acrobatreader/win/2.x/

Installing and Using Adobe Acrobat™

To install under Windows 95, double click on the downloaded file "acroread.exe," or use the Run function under the Start button. In either case, the Acrobat Reader installs quickly and easily. It produces one icon, which launches the Acrobat Reader. Once launched, Acrobat works much like any writing program. You will see a blank window with a toolbar above it. Use the "File" section on the toolbar in order to open a file. The Acrobat reader will read any file with a ".pdf" file extension.

Index